TRANSPORT

NEW WOLSEY THEATRE

A Transport/New Wolsey Theatre co-production

INVISIBLE

by Tena Štivičić

D0995525

First performed at the New Wolsey Theatre, Ipswich, on 13 October 2011

Originally developed at the National Theatre Studio, London

This production is supported by

LOTTERY FUNDED

European
Cultural
Foundation

SUBSIDISED REHEARSAL FACILITIES PROVIDED BY

JERWOOD SPACE

THE UNIVERSITY OF
WINCHESTER

A Transport/New Wolsey Theatre co-production

INVISIBLE

by Tena Štivičić

Cast

Dane/Stefan/George	Liam Bergin
Lara	Anna Elijasz
Felix	Jon Foster
Anton	Krystian Godlewski
Leyla/Louise	Gracy Goldman
Mykola/Malik/Gerry	Mark Jax
Ann/Sera	Bridgitta Roy

All other parts played by members of the company

Director	Douglas Rintoul
Choreographer	Darren Johnston
Designer	Hayley Grindle
Lighting Designer	Katharine Williams
Sound Designer	Emma Laxton
Dramaturg	Synne K. Behrndt
Producer/Company Stage Manager	Emma Cameron
Production Manager	Ben Payne for Illuminate Design
Technical Manager	Tim Middleton
Costume Supervisor	Lucy Jane Martin
Re-lights	Rowan Pashley for Illuminate Design
Props	Beatrice Cockburn
Tour Booker	Michael Brazier
Press	Ben Clare Theatre & Dance PR
Set Build	Mercury Theatre Workshops, Colchester
Set Electrics	Illuminate Design
Photography/Film	Zbigniew Kotkiewicz

Far and Near

'I like to bring things down to a human scale,' says an opportunistic businessman in *Invisible*. At the other end of the spectrum a man who has fled his country remarks that even a frown from strangers 'makes me feel like I still have flesh'. In *Invisible* we meet people from very different backgrounds, with different status in society and very different scale of problems. Their circumstances are vastly different yet they are connected through the same predicament; the challenge for them all is to find stable ground, a sense of purpose, and to make sense of a world that is *on the move*.

Migration is changing the shape of the world, and as Suárez-Orozco remarks at the 'turn of the millennium, an estimated 175 million transnational immigrants and refugees were living beyond their homelands.'[1] This extraordinary number of people moving across space is literally changing the world. For some the journey is about being able to live without fear, for others it is the pursuit of better life prospects. As John Berger writes: 'Month by month, millions leave their homelands. They leave because there is nothing there, except their everything, which does not offer enough to feed their children. Once it did. This is the poverty of the new capitalism.'[2]

In his lecture 'Of Other Spaces' (1967), the French theorist Michel Foucault said that above all we live in an epoch of space where our experience of life is that of 'a network that connects the points'. We live, he remarks, in an 'epoch of the near and far.'[3] This suggestion that the world be seen in terms of a network where the 'far' and the 'near' are interlocked, begins to make sense when one notices the way in which changes occurring in communities in one part of the world have a profound impact on communities in other parts of the world. Economic migration is therefore not merely about people in faraway places, it is also about the mechanisms that have created an enormous inequality in our world, and the way in which this inequality impacts on all levels of our society. Suárez-Orozco points out that 'Globalisation's discontent also visits the "other half": the wealthy, advanced, postindustrial democracies, which have, arguably benefited the most under its reign.'[4]

Invisible attempts to imagine the faces, the bodies and the individual human experiences, the 'human scale' behind the statistics. Who are the people who leave their homelands month by month and find themselves in a new and disorientating context? And how may their experience be juxtaposed with the human consequences for globalisation's 'other half'? Finally, how does living in a world on the move shape the individual sense of identity and belonging?

Synne K. Behrndt
Dramaturg

1. Chapter 'Right Moves? Immigration, Globalization, Utopia, and Dystopia', in *The New Immigration. An Interdisciplinary Reader* (eds. Marcelo and Carola Suárez-Orozco and Desirée Qin, Brunner-Routledge 2005, p.7)

2. John Berger: 'Hold Everything Dear: dispatches on survival and resistance', Verso, 2008, p.114.

3. http://foucault.info/documents/heteroTopia/foucault.heteroTopia.en.html (last accessed 24/09/2011/12.08pm)

4. Chapter 'Right Moves? Immigration, Globalization, Utopia, and Dystopia', in *The New Immigration. An Interdisciplinary Reader* (eds. Marcelo and Carola Suárez -Orozco and Desirée Qin, Brunner-Routledge 2005, p.4)

Cast and Crew Biographies

Synne K. Behrndt   Dramaturg
Synne Behrndt is a dramaturg, lecturer and researcher. Synne has worked as a dramaturg for various dance theatre and devising companies in the UK and Denmark. In the UK she has worked as dramaturg with David Harradine and Fevered Sleep on *An Infinite Line: Brighton* (Brighton Festival, 2008), and *On Ageing* (Young Vic, 2010); Platform4 on *The Tempest* (UK tour 2009), choreographer Cathy Seago on *DUOD* (UK tour 2010). Synne has published texts on performance: *Dramaturgy and Performance* co-written with Cathy Turner; a chapter on People Show in *Devising in Process* (eds. Jackie Smart and Alex Mermikides); and has most recently co-edited a special issue of *Contemporary Theatre Review* on 'New Dramaturgies'. She has been an invited speaker and chairperson at dramaturgy events in Tel Aviv, Warsaw, Slovenia and Denmark. Synne is co-founder of the performance collective Secret Hotel, based in Århus, Denmark, and lectures in Performing Arts at the University of Winchester.

Liam Bergin   *Dane/Stefan/George*
Liam trained at Guildhall School of Music and Drama. Theatre includes: *The Marriage of Figaro* (Watermill); *The Will of Fortune* (Theatre503); *Stench* (LIT Ensemble); *Much Ado About Nothing* (Chester Performs); *Romeo and Juliet* (Exeter Northcott/Ludlow Festival); *Semi-Monde, Plenty, The London Cuckholds, The Winter's Tale, Hamlet, The Full Monty, Oedipus Rex, The Importance of Being Earnest, The City Wives Confederacy, Three Sisters* (Guildhall). Television includes: *EastEnders, Doctors* (BBC); *Minder* (Talkback Thames); *Trinity* (Roughcut, ITV).

Emma Cameron   Producer
Emma trained at Rose Bruford College. Emma is the Producer for TRANSPORT and a freelance stage manager. Stage management includes: *Shun-kin, A Disappearing Number, Measure for Measure* and *A Minute Too Late* (Complicite); *The Wasteland* (Wilton's Music Hall and international tour); *Happy Days* (National Theatre and international tour); *Mother Courage, The Rose Tattoo, Connections 2011* (National Theatre); *Aunt Dan and Lemon, Drunk Enough To Say I Love You?, Woman and Scarecrow* and *Motortown* (Royal Court); *Hamlet* and *The Taming of the Shrew* (Theatre Royal Plymouth/UK tour).

Beatrice Cockburn   Props
Bea trained at the Guildhall School of Music and Drama, specialising in Props and Scenic Art. Since graduating in 2009 she has predominantly worked as a Prop Maker, for various productions, including *Sister Act* (West End), *Alice in Wonderland* (Scottish Ballet), and themed attractions including Ripley's Believe It Or Not and the London Dungeon. Recently she also made samba costumes for the London School of Samba at Notting Hill Carnival and Thames Festival, and worked as Assistant Stage Manager in

charge of props and costume maintenance for *On the Record* (Arcola). Bea
has also worked as a prop maker and stylist on photoshoots for The
Paperboat Creative and Getty Images.

Anna Elijasz   *Lara*
Anna trained at Guildhall School of Music and Drama and is making her
professional stage debut in *Invisible*. Productions whilst training include:
*Summerfolk, When Five Years Pass,The Astonished Heart, Curtains, A
Midsummer Night's Dream, Don Juan in Soho, King Lear, The Women of
Troy, Little Me, The Relapse, Far Away, Three Sisters, Rabbit.*

Jon Foster   *Felix*
Jon trained at East 15 Acting School. Theatre includes: *Dream Story, Mud*
(Gate); *The Alchemist, Firehouse, How to Tell the Monsters from the Misfits*
(Birmingham Rep); Dog in *Long Time Dead* (Paines Plough/Traverse); *Food*
(Imaginary Body/Traverse); *After Haggerty* (Finborough); *A New Way to
Please You*; *Speaking Like Magpies, Sejanus, Thomas Moore* (RSC); *Free
from Sorrow* (Tristan Bates); *Romeo and Juliet* (Creation); *The Melancholy
Hussar, Oliver Twist* (Etcetera); *The Two Gentlemen of Verona*
(Pentameters). Television includes: *Come Rain or Shine, Law & Order,
EastEnders, IT Crowd, The Bill, Clone, Instinct, Silent Witness.* Film includes:
Nice Guy, Love's Kitchen, Abroad, The Orchard, Still Moving.

Krystian Godlewski   *Anton*
Krystian trained at the Theatrical Academy in Warsaw, Public Studies of
Culture Animation in Gdansk, Fine Arts College. Other training includes:
Academy of Gardzienice Theatre; Witkacy Theatre from Zakopane; butoh
dance with Mikka Takeuchi and Itto Morita, Marie-Gabriel Rotie; puppetry
with Department of Puppetry Art in Bialystok, Grotowski training with
Hairo Cuesta, James Slowiak from New World Performance Laboratory,
Canada and Marcin Rudy from Song of the Goat. He has been a member of
Stajnia Pegaza Theatre, Sopot, for seven years and has worked with the
Alternative Scene, Off de Bicz in Sopot, Zak' Student Club in Gdansk,
Culture and International Co-operation Centre in Elblag, Terminus A Quo
Theatre, Nowa Sol.

Gracy Goldman   *Leyla/Louise*
Gracy trained at RADA. Theatre includes: Iras in *Antony and Cleopatra*
(Liverpool Playhouse); *Dream of the Dog* (Trafalgar Studios); *The Lost Voice*
(Royal Festival Hall); *Re:Design* (Menagerie/University of Toronto); *Egusi
Soup* (Menagerie); *Great Expectations* (New Vic); *You Can't Take It with You*
(Southwark Playhouse); *Chasing the Moment* (Arcola); *Quabaka* (Oval
Playhouse); *Beautiful Thing* (Leicester Haymarket); *Broken Voices* (New
Company); *The Tempest* (Theatre Royal, Bury St Edmunds); *Othello* (Good
Company); *The Sneeze* (Good Company); *Pericles* (RSC); *The Tempest* (RSC);
The Winter's Tale (RSC); and *An Enchanted Land* (Riverside Studios). Film and
television credits include: *The Plant, Doctors, Casualty* (BBC); *The Bill* (ITV);
The Detectives (Cedar Productions); *Ruth Rendell Mysteries* (Blue Heaven
Productions); *Auf Eigene Gefahr* (Regina/Zeigler TV); and *Metamorphosis*.

Hayley Grindle   Designer

Hayley trained at the Royal Welsh College of Music and Drama where she received the Paul Kimpton Prize for Innovation. Theatre includes: *God in Ruins* (RSC); *Animal Farm* (Peter Hall Company); *The Nutcracker, Around the World in Eighty Days, His Dark Materials, A Midsummer's Night Dream, Ben Hur* and *Blue Room* (Theatre Royal Bath); *My Mother Said I Never Should, Peter Pan, The Rise and Fall of Little Voice* (Dukes, Lancaster); *Travels with My Aunt* (New Wolsey, Ipswich); *King Lear* (Creation/BMW Plant); *The Gentlemen's Tea Drinking Society* (Ransom Productions, Belfast); *Two Shakespearean Actors* and *A Midsummer's Night Dream* (Guildhall School of Music and Drama); *Ghetto* and *Great Expectations* (Watford Palace); *All the Way Home* (Manchester Library); *The Mikado* (Welsh National Opera, Youth Opera); *A Day to Remember* and *Mongrel Island* (Soho); *Muscle* (Bristol Old Vic); *Treasure Island* (Watermill, Newbury).

Darren Johnston   Choreographer

Darren Johnston is artistic director of Array. He trained at Laban and graduated with the outstanding Choreographic Achievement Award. With his first professional work he won first prizes at major international choreography competitions, including the International Choreographen Concours in Groningen, Holland. He was also awarded the Bonnie Bird Choreography Award. His full-scale installation *Ren-sa*, beginning with a magical, mystery bus tour, was given a Herald Angel Award at the Edinburgh Festival Fringe 2005. Darren's explorative collaborations have led him to work with artists such as Squarepusher, Jamie Lidell and Christian Vogel. In 2005 he choreographed the stage show for the one-off Aphex Twin/Chris Cunningham show in Turin and opened for the Warp Moves show at Brighton Dome. Darren is a former associate artist at The Place and of the Southbank Centre. Darren was recently artist-in-residence at the Roundhouse, London, creating *Underdrome*, the first site-specific work for the iconic main space.

Illuminate Design

Illuminate Design is a production management and technical support company focused on bringing quality support and guidance to theatrical production. With over forty-five years combined experience, working with some of the largest dance and theatre companies in the UK, illuminate provide access to a range of products and services to assist production companies with any scale of production from site-specific performances to large-scale international tours. Along with providing technical support, Illuminate also supply skilled and dedicated technicians and designers to fulfill project needs, all of whom are used to working in the live-performance sector. Recent clients include: Jasmin Vardimon Dance Company, Havana Rakatan for Sadler's Wells, Protein Dance, Tilted Productions, ATC Productions, Frauke Requardt, Yorke Dance, London Studio Centre, Henri Oguike Dance Company, London International Festival of Theatre (LIFT), South East Dance, The School Creative Centre, Rye, Bourne Leisure, Mayor's Thames Festival. More information is available at: www.illuminatedesign.co.uk

Mark Jax *Mykola/Malik/Gerry*

Mark trained at RADA under Hugh Crutwell. Theatre includes: *The Three Musketeers* (Traverse/Coventry/ETT); *Fast Labour* (Hampstead/West Yorkshire Playhouse); *Rough Crossings* (Headlong); *Mirror for Princes* (Barbican/tour); *Jamaica Inn, Barbarians, The Norma Conquests* (Salisbury Playhouse); *Season's Greetings* (Mill at Sonning); *Prophet in Exile* (Chelsea Centre); *Laughter on the 23rd Floor* (Queen's West End/tour); *Mansfield Park* (Chichester Festival Theatre); *The Way of the World, Macbeth, The Tenant of Wildfell Hall, Peter Pan, The Atheist's Tragedy, Romeo and Juliet, Rope, Women Beware Women* (Birmingham Rep); *Romeo and Juliet, Mansfield Park* (Crucible, Sheffield); *The Devils* (Theatre Clwyd); *A Christmas Carol* (Young Vic); *Strange Kind of Animal, Pravda, The Government Inspector, A Midsummer Night's Dream, The Futurists* (National Theatre); *A Chorus of Disapproval, The Dresser, The Westwoods and I, Bricks and Mortars, The Linden Tree* (Stephen Joseph); *Two Planks and a Passion* (Northcott Exeter). Television: *Marco Polo* (Polo Productions); *Frankenstein* (Silverstar Ltd); *Doctors, Casualty, A View From the Bridge, The Road to 1984, Most Dangerous Man in the World, Wuffer, Grange Hill* (BBC); *The Vice IV* (Carlton Television); *The Bill* (Pearson Television); *In the Beginning, Mary and Jesus, Merlin* (Hallmark Productions); *Family Affairs* (Channel Five); *The Two of Us, Not a Penny More, Not a Penny Less* (LWT); *Shake Hands Forever* (TVS); *The Perfect Match* (Granada); *Picture of Woman* (Channel 4); *Tales of the Unexpected* (Anglia TV). Film: *Desi Boyz* (Desi Boyz ltd); *Stealing Heaven* (Amy International); *Living Doll* (Spectacular Films).

Emma Laxton Sound Designer

Theatre includes: *Much Ado About Nothing* (Wyndhams); *One Monkey Don't Stop No Show* (Eclipse/Sheffield); *Where's My Seat, The Whisky Taster, If There Is I Haven't Found It Yet, Like a Fishbone, Apologia, 2000 Feet Away* (Bush); *The Heretic* (Royal Court); *Precious Little Talent* (Trafalgar Studios); *Charged* (Clean Break/Soho); *Men Should Weep* (Lyttelton, National Theatre); *My Romantic History* (Sheffield/Bush); *Travels With My Aunt* (Northampton Royal); *Sisters* (Crucible Studio); *Timing* (King's Head); *Ghosts* (ATC, Arcola); *Treasure Island* (Theatre Royal Haymarket); *Pornography* (Birmingham Rep/Traverse); *Europe* (Transport/Dundee Rep/Barbican Pit); *Other Hands* (Soho); for the Royal Court: *Off The Endz!, Tusk, Tusk, Faces in the Crowd, That Face* (and West End), *My Name is Rachel Corrie* (and Playhouse/Minetta Lane, New York). Emma is the Associate Sound Designer for *War Horse*.

Lucy Jane Martin Costume Supervisor

Lucy trained at Rose Bruford College and now works as a costume supervisor and assistant. Her recent work in theatre includes: *The Veil, London Assurance, The Eternal Knot* and *St Joan* (National Theatre); *Crazy for You, The Beggar's Opera, Lord of the Flies, Into the Woods, The Comedy of Errors* and *The Crucible* (Regents Park Open Air Theatre); and *La Bohème* (English National Opera). As an alterations hand and costume maker she has worked with various film, television and theatre companies as well as a independent commissions.

Tim Middleton   Technical Manager
Tim graduated from the Guildhall School of Music and Drama in 2009 with
a degree in Technical Theatre and having specialised in Sound. Recent
sound design credits include: *The Exonerated* (Charing Cross); *Wet
Weather Cover* (King's Head and transfer to Arts Theatre); *The Spanish
Tragedy* (Arcola); *The Last Five Years* (Barbican Pit). He has also worked on
various productions for the National Theatre, Barbican Theatre, Cheek By
Jowl, HighTide Festival and Pentabus.

Douglas Rintoul   Director
Douglas is the Artistic Director of Transport and a freelance theatre
director who has directed for the Barbican, Trafalgar Studios, Dundee
Rep Theatre, Les Théâtres de la Ville de Luxembourg, National Theatre
Studio, Salisbury Playhouse, New Wolsey Theatre, Creation, Central
School of Speech and Drama, and Guildhall School of Music and Drama.
He is also a long-standing associate director to Simon McBurney/
Complicite and an assistant and associate director to Deborah Warner.
He won a prestigious Channel 4 Theatre Director Scheme bursary and an
Esmeé Fairbairn Regional Theatre Initiative award. For Transport: *Europe*
and *The Edge*.

Tena Štivičić   Writer
Tena Štivičić was born in Croatia. She holds a BA in Dramaturgy from the
Academy of Drama Art in Zagreb and an MA in Writing for Performance
from Goldmsiths College, University of London. Her plays *Can't Escape
Sundays* (2000), *At Deathbed* (1998), *The Two of Us* (2002), *Fragile!*
(2004), *Fireflies* (2007), *Felix* (2008) and plays for children *Perceval – the
Quest for the Grail* (2001) and *Psssst!* (2004) have been produced and
published in a number of European countries and translated and
published in many languages. They won numerous awards including
Marin Držić Award for best play of the year 2000 for *Can't Escape
Sundays*, Best Play for the production of *Fragile!* at Borstnikova Srecanja
in Slovenia 2007, European Authors Award and Innovation Award at
Heidelberg Stueckemarkt in Germany 2008 for *Fragile!*, Best Play at
Marulićevi Dani Festival in Croatia 2008 for *Fireflies*, a play devised at the
National Theatre Studio in London. In 2007 she wrote a one-act play as
part of omnibus of plays entitled *Goldoni Terminus*, premiered at the
Venice Biennale. She co-created two plays for the Ulysses Theatre in
Croatia, *Drunken Night 1918*, and *Romeo and Juliet 1968*, and continues
to work with Ulysses Theatre as the theatre dramaturg. As part of 'The
50' – a Royal Court Theatre and BBC initiative to mark the fiftieth
anniversary of Royal Court Theatre, she was nominated as one of the fifty
most promising young writers in Great Britain. Her columns from the
magazine *Zaposlena* in Croatia were published as a book in 2007, and
made the top of the non-fiction charts. Her play *Seven Days in Zagreb*
was the Croatian partner in the ETC Orient Express international project
in summer 2009. Tena is currently under commission with the
Birmingham Repertory Theatre. She lives in London and writes in English
and Croatian.

Bridgitta Roy *Ann/Sera*
Bridgitta trained at the Royal Welsh College of Music and Drama. Theatre credits include: *Romeo and Juliet* (Shakespeare's Globe); *A Midsummer Night's Dream, The American Pilot* (RSC); *The Travels of Three English Brothers* (National Theatre Studio/British Museum); *Gaddafi: A Living Myth* (ENO); *Jack and the Beanstalk* (Theatre Royal Stratford East); *Macbeth* (Chester Gateway); *Arabian Nights* (Dukes, Lancaster); *The Glass Slipper* (Southwark Playhouse); *Tall Storeys* (Lyric Hammersmith); *The Tale of the Anklet* (National Theatre); *Lords and Ladies* (London Bubble); *Safar, The Sea that Blazed* (Made in Wales); *La Gioconda* (Edinburgh Festival). Television credits include: *Holby City, Dalziel and Pascoe, EastEnders, Casualty.* Film work includes: *Bass Odyssey, Loose Change.* Bridgitta also works as a director in opera and music theatre. As a member of the teaching staff at Guildhall School of Music and Drama, she specialises in working with singers from undergraduate to postgraduate level. She also coaches at the National Opera Studio.

Katharine Williams Lighting Designer
Katharine works in drama, dance and physical theatre, with some opera, musical and circus projects. Her designs have been seen in China, Hong Kong, New Zealand, Canada, the USA, Mexico, Ireland, Holland, Spain, Italy, Germany, Luxembourg, Armenia, Romania, Russia and the Czech Republic as well as the UK. Recent designs include: *The Goat (or Who is Sylvia?)* (Traverse Theatre); *Migrations* (Circus Space, London); *Closer* (Les Théâtres de la Ville de Luxembourg); *Not I* (South Bank Centre); *Underdrome* (Roundhouse, London); *Amgen: Broken* (Sherman Theatre Cymru, Cardiff); *Dolls* (National Theatre of Scotland); *I Am Falling* (Sadler's Wells). Katharine is co-director of Daedalus.

Transport would like to thank the following: Phillip Arditti, Hannah Bentley, Michelle Bonnard, Claire Brown, Cristina Catalina, Complicite, Gergo Danka, The Dover Detainee Volunteer Group, Hannes Flaschberger, Thusitha Jayasundera, Douglas Henshall, Phil Hurley @ Stage Sound Services, The Jerwood Space, Gareth Kennerly, Pieter Lawman, Brian Lonsdale, Tommy Luther, Anamaria Marinca, The National Theatre Studio, Sarah Niles, Magdalena Poplawska, Philip Rham, Finn Ross, Nick Scott-Flynn (Red Cross), Anthony Shuster, Serge Soric, Ben Noble @Stage Electrics, Fiona Stewart, Marko Turcich, Lucia Tong, Vince Virr, Maya Wasowicz, The University of Winchester, Alexander Wolpert.

TRANSPORT

Theatre Without Borders

TRANSPORT is an international arts company based on the south-east coast of England that exists to make work, which celebrates the diversity of the human experience, engages the imagination and promotes new theatrical forms and collaborations.

TRANSPORT's first project was a revival of David Greig's 1994 play *Europe*. It was co-produced by Barbican International Theatre Events (BITE) in London, and Dundee Repertory Theatre in Scotland. TRANSPORT recently premiered *Elegy* in a gallery space at the Edinburgh Festival Fringe 2011; this devised piece was inspired by interviews with gay Iraqi refugees in exile in Syria. Earlier this year TRANSPORT worked with third-year collaborative and devised theatre students at Central School of Speech and Drama, London, exploring ideas for a new piece centered on narratives of migration in relationship to climate change. This project is a collaboration with Kolkata-based dance/theatre company RANAN. TRANSPORT will travel to India and Bangladesh in 2011/2012 to develop the project. This work is supported by the British Council.

In the summer of 2011, TRANSPORT launched an interdisciplinary arts platform, *LOW&HIGH*, based in an empty shop in the Creative Quarter of east Folkestone, Kent. For three months the *LOW&HIGH* space was used as a rehearsal space, artist-in-residence studio, and a venue for workshops, presentations and discussions exploring the connections between the arts (theatre and visual art) and geography, sociology and politics. This programme of work formed part of the Folkestone Triennial Fringe.

TRANSPORT is headed by director Douglas Rintoul and producer Emma Cameron.

To be kept in touch about future performances, sharings, readings and workshops join our mailing list or find us on Facebook and/or Twitter.

admin@transport-theatre.eu
www.transport-theatre.eu
twitter.com/transporttheatr

Board of Directors: Katrina Edwards, David Harradine, Declan Pollock and Robbie MacDonald

Charity Number: 1140196 **Company Registration Number:** 6890210

The New Wolsey produces and presents a year-round programme of work for all ages in both the theatre (400 seats) and the studio (106 seats), combining its own productions with a wide range of visiting theatre, music, comedy and other performing arts.

Nationally renowned for its producing work, both as a sole producer and in collaboration with a diverse range of UK artists and companies, in recent years, the theatre has co-produced with other regional theatres – Clwyd Theatr Cymru, Salisbury Playhouse, Colchester Mercury – touring companies such as Graeae, Talawa, Tiata Fahodzi, Eclipse Theatre, and commercial producers like Avalon and Mark Goucher Ltd. The theatre has a particular reputation for musical work, often employing actor-musicians, and is increasingly acknowledged as a leading player in the development of new musicals, staging the world premieres of *It's A Wonderful Life* and *20th Century Boy*.

The New Wolsey has also established a reputation for artist development, and in particular helping to nurture innovative companies and enabling them to produce work designed for the middle scale. As part of this development programme, the New Wolsey has worked in association with some of the most exciting and innovative companies in the UK and internationally, including in recent years, Hoipolloi Theatre Company, Analogue Theatre Company, Gecko, LOT Teatro (Peru) and now, TRANSPORT.

In this, the tenth anniversary year of the New Wolsey Theatre, we have been awarded a new agreement from the Arts Council as a National Portfolio Organisation, as have our associate company, Gecko; Analogue have just been awarded a Fringe First at the Edinburgh Fringe Festival; building work is currently taking place at the back of our studio theatre, where another building, the HEG, is being converted and refurbished to house our expanding creative-learning programme, and we are in conversations with other theatres and producers about the further exploitation of previous productions. Not bad for a ten-year-old.

This success comes as a result of the support we have received for all aspects of our programme, from funding bodies, partner organisations, volunteers and, most importantly, individual participants and audience members.

Peter Rowe
Artistic Director

Bridgitta Roy, Krystian Godlewski, Liam Bergin, Jon Foster, Mark Jax, Anna Elijasz, Gracy Goldman
Photograph © Zbigniew Kotkiewicz

Tena Štivičić with Jon Foster, Mark Jax and Bridgitta Roy
Photograph © Zbigniew Kotkiewicz

INVISIBLE

Tena Štivičić

For Dougie

Author thanks

I would like to thank Douglas Rintoul and Emma Cameron at Transport, Synne K. Behrndt, Sarah Holmes and Peter Rowe at the New Wolsey Theatre, Purni Morell and the National Theatre Studio and everyone who took the time to speak to me during my research.

This play was inspired by the extraordinary book *A Seventh Man* by John Berger and Jean Moir.

Characters

FORTRESS EUROPE
FELIX, *male, thirties*
ANN, *female, thirties*
GERRY, *male, thirties*
LOUISE, *female, forties*
GEORGE, *male, forties*
THERAPIST, *male or female, forties*
BOY 1, *teenager*
BOY 2, *teenager*

THE OTHERS
ANTON, *male, thirties*
LARA, *female, twenties*
STEFAN, *male, thirties*
LEYLA, *female, teens*
SERA, *female, forties*
MALIK, *male, forties*
CLEANER, *female, thirties*

MYKOLA, *male, sixties*
DANE, *male, thirties*

Staff, officers, interviewers, passers-by

This text went to press before the end of rehearsals and so may differ slightly from the play as performed.

I

FELIX. Something happened. A thing. An incident. Something I could have stopped. Something I may not have been able to stop. The point is – I'm not the point. There are these... forces at play. And I don't mean 'dark' forces. I'm not insane. In fact, I don't like that word. It's patronising. What is sanity, surely you must wonder about that. Isn't it merely a social construct? I mean, where is the line between a chemical imbalance and pure social impropriety? Anyway, what I meant was, there are greater forces at play. Wider, social, historical, political forces. One finds oneself entangled in a situation created by the convergence of all these forces and one faces a question – the sequence of events, whatever it was, was it meant to happen? Should I have acted on an impulse and tried to change it? Do you know what I mean?

Silence as FELIX*'s* THERAPIST *gazes at him.*

Do you think I'm a good man?

A Long, Long Kitchen Table

FELIX *sits at his long kitchen table, distraught.* ANN *stands next to him. Almost like a mother towering over a son.*

ANN. What have you done?

FELIX *is silent.*

What have you done to us?

FELIX. I'm sorry.

ANN. You're sorry?

Silence.

You're sorry?

FELIX. Yes.

Silence.

ANN. Is it that you are bored? Felix? Is it that you're unhappy? Is it… What is it?

FELIX. No. I don't know. I can't explain.

ANN. You can't explain.

FELIX. No.

ANN. He can't explain. What am I supposed to do with that?

Silence.

Have you thought of me at all? Have you… thought of me?

FELIX. I have.

ANN. And what, I don't understand, you see, if you thought of me then…

FELIX. In fact, if I hadn't thought of you, it probably would have played out differently. I probably would have stayed…

A Hospital

ANTON *is lying in a hospital bed, hooked to a machine, unconscious.*

A CLEANER *carefully enters. She looks around. She then lets* LARA *in the room.*

CLEANER. You know him?

LARA. Yes.

CLEANER. Handsome man. But what's it worth, lying here.

LARA. He's not dead.

CLEANER. You should tell the doctors then. They don't even know his name.

LARA *is silent.*

Okay. None of my business. If they ask you, I don't know you. Okay? I don't want to lose my job.

LARA. Okay. Thank you.

CLEANER. Hey. You never know. He might still wake up.

The CLEANER *leaves.* LARA *pulls up a chair to the bed. She takes a seat. She strokes* ANTON*'s hand. She sits there in silence.*

*

FELIX. Did you know that there was a theory that we all come from one and the same African tribe? Seventy thousand years ago they started a first-ever migration. From Kenya. I think. Or somewhere around there. And all of us alive today can trace our ancestry back to that one tribe. Isn't that fascinating? So, I've been thinking, these past few days, you know, with all the events that took place and I'm not saying I'm a victim, I mean I'm not trying to shed accountability, but you know how we all found ourselves in each other's way is really... not a conscious choice. Do you understand? So many choices are made for us. Don't you think? I think I could have been happy being a miller, for instance. In a different time. Look at you, for example, this nice house in this nice neighbourhood and this lovely office with this wonderful designer chair, is this Formica? That would not have been possible, if we lived in a less fucked-up time, wouldn't you agree?

ANN. Felix, I don't understand what you are on about. Christ, can't you just talk to me?

THERAPIST. And how do you see these historical forces affecting your actions?

Pause.

FELIX. Well, it's not an easy thing to know, is it? I'm trying to give it a context, I'm trying to give myself a context.

He stops. He takes a breath.

I guess if I choose to look at things that way I would have to come to the conclusion that this is probably their story more than it is mine. Which is another rather depressing benchmark. Being a supporting character in one's own life.

THERAPIST. Is that how you feel? Like a supporting character?

FELIX. Yes. Sometimes. People feel like that...

THERAPIST. What makes you feel like that?

Pause.

FELIX. We're running around in circles here, aren't we?

THERAPIST. Are we?

*

LARA. 'There once was a man and he had a son and a daughter. He was so poor that when the children grew up he summoned them and said: "Children, I am a poor man and I have nothing to give you with which to start a life of your own. Go off to the world and find your happiness".' All the stories where I come from begin like that. 'And the children set out, there's no other choice and the great unknown besets them. But no sooner did they leave, they happen upon a golden bird.' Sometimes it's a golden goose. (*Pause.*) In all my time away I have never happened upon any golden poultry. And neither have you.

Silence.

I'm sure... I'm sure he's a good man. It's the eyes, I think. He's the only... he's the first Englishman... whose eyes smile. At me.

Silence.

'And the father said to his son: "There is a land far away where gold lies in the streets. Follow the wind, let it carry you. Where the wind drops you, that's where you start to search for your happiness. Beware of dangers and temptations. Beware of the Klek Mountain where the wind howls and the witches dance. But I know you'll know what to do. Go, son. Tread wisely." And the man went.'

Leaving

A well-appointed village house.

DANE *and* MYKOLA *sit at the kitchen table.* ANTON *brings a bottle of rakia and puts it on the table. He pours two glasses.*

DANE. Aren't you going to join us?

ANTON. I have work to do.

DANE. Busy bee. Our Anton. Always working.

   ANTON's *face stays still. He doesn't break eye contact but he says nothing.*

   You always seemed to prefer your own company, huh? Why is that?

ANTON. I just like to work.

DANE. Yes. People always need furniture. (*Pause.*) Well... not always...

   An ominous silence.

   Join us. (*Pause.*) Come on.

   ANTON *looks at his father. Then unwillingly he pours himself a glass. They raise their glasses and drink.*

   Still the best.

MYKOLA. The plums are sour this year.

DANE. Still you manage to make a good bottle, Mykola. Hands of gold, eh? Isn't that what Ms Mara used to say, rest her soul?

MYKOLA. Yes. That's what she used to say.

DANE. Yes. Like father, like son. Hands of gold. Ever since we were kids. Do you remember, Anton? Good with a basketball, good on the pitch. Good with tools, good with paint. I wonder if you'd be any good with a pistol?

MYKOLA. Let's hope he never has to find out.

DANE. Yes. Let's. I suppose one thing you weren't great with was girls. Why is that? How come you never married?

Silence.

ANTON. You know why. Dane.

DANE. Surely you don't still carry a grudge... Plenty of other fish in the sea.

ANTON*'s face tightens.*

MYKOLA. Let's have another drink and let bygones be bygones.

They pour another glass.

Dane... What's on your mind?

Long pause. DANE *revels in it.*

DANE. I have come to tell you, as a friend and neighbour, to pack your things and go. (*Pause.*) You know what is about to happen.

MYKOLA. I don't believe it.

DANE. Believe what you like, I am telling you how it is. From tomorrow, things are going to change around here. There will be no need for carpentry.

Pause.

MYKOLA. This is my land. My wife is buried here. My daughter is in that convent in the hills, you know that.

DANE *shrugs as though there is nothing he can do.*

I have known you since the day you were born.

DANE. Which is why I have come here to tell you this. I don't want to see my neighbours come to any harm.

Silence.

Well, I better be on my way. Let you pack. (*Pause.*) Piece of advice – travel light.

DANE *leaves.*

MYKOLA *and* ANTON *sit at the table. They sit in silence for a long time, unable to make a move.*

ANTON. We have to go.

MYKOLA nods. But he doesn't move. ANTON looks around the room as if trying to work out what next. He gets up and leaves the room.

Deep in thought, MYKOLA still sits at the table, quietly stroking it.

This goes on for a long minute.

ANTON comes in. He sits down, lost and useless.

I don't know what to pack. (*Pause.*) Where would we go, anyway?

MYKOLA slowly pours them another glass each and passes one to ANTON.

MYKOLA. You'll take a backpack. A suitcase will be clunky to carry. Take warm clothes – in case you have to go up to the mountains.

ANTON. Dad –

MYKOLA. Listen to me –

ANTON. Dad –

MYKOLA. Do as I say!

ANTON. If I go, you go.

MYKOLA. Son, let's not part arguing.

ANTON. If you stay –

Pause.

MYKOLA. I know.

Silence.

Listen, son. We have had our differences. That's what fathers and sons do. I have never been one for much talk but...
There are things that need to be said. I can't go. I have spent too many years out there. It takes a young man... A young man can handle it. Around here, a man works his whole life just so he could afford a funeral. Don't get me wrong, it's no

small thing, a decent funeral. But I wanted more. Just a little bit more. A nice house. A place for Mara and me to spend our last days. I fancied some grandchildren around. For that I was away when you were growing up. And I was away when your mother died. Isn't life funny? Now I am here and I'm on my own. Your sister made that crazy deal with God and she's not very likely to give me grandchildren. The house is finally finished. A big, finished, empty house I worked my whole life for and missed my whole life for. And now they want to take it away from me. Piss in it, shit in it, thrash it and burn it down.

ANTON. It might not come to that.

MYKOLA. It will. This is the best house in the street.

ANTON. Dad –

MYKOLA. But when they come, they will have to burn me down with it. I am not going anywhere.

Silence.

ANTON. Dad –

MYKOLA. I know, son. But you have a whole life ahead of you. You will go and you will put it to good use. There will be images you will never be able to get rid of. You might learn to understand why your uncle Toma did what they say he did. But you will have a chance. A chance is all a man needs.

Interviews I

STEFAN. The journey started unexpectedly.

SERA. A person makes plans. A person spends a lot of time making plans. All sorts of plans. One day, the world turns upside down and you realise there was one plan you never took the time to make.

ANTON. In 1906. My great-grandfather and his best friend travelled days on a donkey to board a ship to America. He was a miller. So they gave him a new name. Joseph Miller. A couple of months later, Joe Miller slipped and fell from the scaffolding on a construction site in Wall Street. His neck broke and he died instantly. His best friend –

STEFAN. My great-grandfather, John Farmer –

ANTON. – was assigned to take his place within two hours of his death.

LARA. It was simple. The moment I knew what I wanted. Where I was going. I was eight and my best friend's mother offered me a Mozart chocolate. I don't know how they got a hold of it. But I thought – this is more wonderful than a dream.

MALIK. I didn't move. My house didn't move. The border moved. Like many times before. But I will go back.

LEYLA. I was born on the road.

Ghost-Town

A shanty town on a coast.

A bunch of PEOPLE *huddle together around barrels with burning fire.*

MALIK. It's going to rain again. Come into my tent.

SERA. No.

MALIK. I've got new rubber sheets on the floor, it's very dry.

SERA. Where did you get them?

MALIK. Found them two days ago. You know the house where they had the funeral the other day?

SERA. Yes.

MALIK. It was the grandmother. Next day they threw out these sheets. I gave them a good rinse, so it's… Well, it smells like rubber more than anything else.

SERA (*excited*). Where? Where did you rinse them?

MALIK. Well… I left them out last night. The rain rinsed them.

SERA*'s spirits fall.*

At least it's not bare ground. It's not right to sleep on bare ground.

SERA *considers.*

SERA. That's nice.

*

ANTON, *newly arrived, and* STEFAN *stand on their own, a little further away.* ANTON *is taking in the surroundings.*

ANTON. How long have you been here?

STEFAN. Twenty-seven days.

ANTON. Twenty-seven days?!

STEFAN. That's nothing. That guy has been here nine months. He has built a hut. There is a girl who tried to get across sixteen times. She's a kid. Just throwing herself in. People have started using her as a decoy. It worked for a few. But it doesn't pay to be hasty. I'm gathering information. I'm waiting for the right moment.

ANTON. I don't understand, why is it so hard?

STEFAN. We're not wanted, Anton. We're not wanted across the Channel, we're not wanted at home, we're not wanted here. It seems like there is no more room. Anywhere.

ANTON. What are we supposed to do?

Silence.

*

MALIK. Why don't you come?

SERA. Malik, I don't want to go into your tent.

MALIK. Would I do anything to you? Sera. You don't trust me?

SERA *is not convinced.*

SERA. What if people see me? I am married.

MALIK. I will protect you. You don't have to care what they say.

SERA. A woman always has to care. That's how it is. Someone is always watching.

MALIK. If you were my wife I wouldn't let you travel alone. I wouldn't let you live like this. I would come and get you.

SERA. That would be very smart of you. Come out of England and then have two people trying to cross instead of one.

MALIK. At least we wouldn't be alone.

*

A WOMAN *is singing a native song. A couple of* PEOPLE *join in, humming.*

ANTON. People can't just stay here. Out in the open.

STEFAN. Look. You can see it from here – the white cliffs – the finish line.

ANTON. And they all want to go to England?

STEFAN. So do you, don't you?

ANTON. I can speak a little bit of the language. I know some of our people are there. I heard good things.

STEFAN. So has everyone.

Silence.

ANTON. Any word from home?

STEFAN. No.

*

A row of phone booths.

An AFRICAN WOMAN *shouts into the phone in one of the booths. In another, a small* CHINESE WOMAN *quietly cries, clutching the receiver.*

LEYLA *waits her turn.*

The CHINESE WOMAN *finishes her call and leaves the booth.*

LEYLA *walks into the booth.*

She dials.

LEYLA. Mama, it's me… how are you? I'm fine. No, I'm not
there yet. I know, I'm trying. I am trying hard. I tried sixteen
times, Mama! I'm not stupid. It's just bad luck. Don't cry.
Please don't cry, I have very little time. No, don't put him on
– Hello, Father. Yes, I am still here. No… I don't have any
more money to give them. No, I can't swim… because it's
too far! Yes, I know I used to, but it's nothing like the river.
Father, please! I'm not raising my voice. The money will run
out. I'll call when I can.

*She hangs up. She looks like she is going to cry. She doesn't
cry.*

*

STEFAN *produces a number of chocolate bars and packets of
biscuits. The* WOMEN *flock towards him and each takes some
chocolate. They start to eat hungrily.* MALIK *looks at him
askance.*

MALIK. Where did you get those?

STEFAN. I rubbed a lamp.

MALIK. It's not right.

STEFAN. Nobody's forcing you to have it.

MALIK. That's how it starts, you know. That's how it starts and
then before you know it, you're… mixed into things… and…
giving us a bad name.

STEFAN. And I suppose you will be flying across first class?

MALIK. I used to be a respected… an outstanding member of
the community. If there was any other way… but as soon as
we get there, I tell you…

STEFAN. Wipe the slate clean and build a respectable life? I
wish you all the best.

He toasts with a chocolate. MALIK *looks at the chocolate, his mouth watering.*

SERA. My husband is over there. He says it rains all the time?

STEFAN. That seems to be true. But it's mild rain and the weather is pleasant all year round.

LEYLA. I heard women walk naked in the streets?

MALIK*'s ears prick up.*

STEFAN. That's true.

MALIK. Completely naked?

STEFAN. No... not completely... half-naked.

SERA *and* LEYLA *look at each other, alarmed.*

LEYLA. Are they forced to walk naked?

STEFAN *is taken aback by the question.*

STEFAN. They... are not forced.

LEYLA. Well, then, why would they –

SERA. Will they make us go naked?

LARA *joins them. Her resolve and conviction make her stand out. She doesn't belong here.* ANTON *notices her and is immediately drawn.*

LARA. They go the way they want to go. Because they're free. It doesn't matter who you are or where you are from. It is full of opportunity. If you work hard and if you are gifted, anything can happen. People get rich and... They have good, comfortable lives.

SERA. My husband says ask for asylum. He says tell your story. Tell everything you know. But... I can't. I just can't remember. It's like in a dream. You are in one place doing one thing and then suddenly you are in a different place doing something else and you don't know how you got there.

MALIK. Does he say anything about gold lying on the ground?

SERA. No.

STEFAN. That's just a saying.

MALIK. I know it's a saying.

STEFAN. Then, what are you asking?

MALIK. You have no respect.

LEYLA. But there are jobs? They say there are good jobs and you can quickly pay off your debts.

LARA. A friend of mine knows a woman who went to work as an au pair. Now she has her own agency. She is the boss. And it's a big business. Another friend knows someone who went to school and became a doctor and is now the most respected doctor in a town, I can't remember the name now.

STEFAN. Yes, I know about that doctor.

LEYLA. How do you know all this?

STEFAN. Information is everything.

SERA. I just want to find my husband. He will know what's to be done.

Silence.

MALIK. I don't think it's true. About those camps.

Silence.

STEFAN. Have a chocolate, man.

MALIK *looks at the chocolate. He struggles for a few moments. He gets up and leaves without it, his dignity intact. He sits further away.*

All I know is, England will be better. It can't be worse.

Bruxelles, Fortress Europe

FELIX *gives a speech at a conference. Graphs and diagrams are projected behind him.*

FELIX. There was an ad a few years ago saying 'the future is bright'. As our awareness of the state our world is in grows literally on a daily basis, I can't imagine any company with half a brain would put out an ad like that today. Because, whether we're sceptics, or campaigners or we simply can't quite get our heads around what the reports and studies have been saying, we all know that 'the future is bright' is not really a likely scenario. I suspect we've all been wondering, in fact, probably fearing what sacrifices lie ahead. Well, I think you'll agree, the surge in figures we have seen in today's reports suggests a very promising way ahead.

Partly as a result of the EU Renewable Electricity Directive of 2001, there has been an almost five-fold increase in the annual market in the past five years confirming that a second wave of European countries are investing in wind power. Eastern Europe has become one of the most promising emerging markets. I would like to take this opportunity to talk about a very exciting new pilot project in Romania, where we plan to build one of the biggest yet wind farms in this part of Europe.

At the Airport

At the airport bar, GERRY *sits comfortably, like a man who spends a lot of his time drinking in airport bars. A glass of whiskey in his hand. He stops* FELIX, *who is passing by.*

GERRY. Good work. Excellent speech today.

FELIX. Ah, thank you. Hello, how are you?

They shake hands.

I would have called but I'm on the 4:50 back to London.

GERRY. That's alright. I'm on the 5:10 to Frankfurt. Can't wait to get out of this dreary place. Can I get you a drink?

FELIX *checks his mobile phone, he looks around, he doesn't really want to stay.*

FELIX. I don't think I have time for a drink. I'll see you in London next week, right? You're coming in for the meeting with the Romanians?

GERRY. Looking forward to it. I hear you might be joining us in Romania?

FELIX. Well, my boss has suggested, but I'm not really looking to relocate.

GERRY. There is a lot of potential there. It's worth considering. And believe me, people don't know this, but it's a blast.

FELIX. You're based in Romania?

GERRY. I'm between Romania and Serbia. Travelling a lot through 'the region'. A quick drink?

FELIX. ... Alright. I'll have sparkling water.

GERRY. Sparkling water?

Unwittingly, or perhaps not at all unwittingly, his tone sounds judgemental.

FELIX. Oh... we're doing this thing. My wife and I. This no-alcohol, no-sugar course.

GERRY. Sounds like fun.

FELIX. It's just a temporary... She's a nutritionist. It's very energising.

GERRY. Sparkling water it is. Are you allowed lemon?

And he laughs at his own joke.

Can we have a sparkling water and another one of these? (*Points to his glass.*) Trust me, you'd love it. London has become over-regulated. Over-monitored. There's no freedom any more.

FELIX. Are you saying there's freedom in Serbia?

GERRY. What I'm saying is, over there, they still know how to have fun. Professionally, the countries are quite barbaric, for sure. Drowning in corruption. Greed is a major factor in all those ex-socialist countries. They want everything now. The are gagging for 'stuff'. You know, multicoloured, shiny 'stuff'. In the past they could choose between various shades of brown and grey. And now, now the colour scheme has opened up in front of them, they want all the colours of the rainbow, no matter what it costs. So, they are looking to make money and they can drive a hard bargain. Still, great, great potential over there. I think the future is looking very exciting.

FELIX. The future of mankind?

GERRY *giggles knowingly.*

GERRY. The future of... men. A number of men. Mankind I find too big an idea to deal with. I like to bring it down to human scale.

FELIX (*half-hearted*). That's wise.

GERRY. Plus they like to eat and drink and party like there's no tomorrow. You'll see.

FELIX. Oh, I don't know. I think my partying days are over.

GERRY. Nonsense. A young man like you. With your talents. Maybe your English partying days are over. This is a whole new world you're about to discover.

FELIX. Is it safe? I mean, is it stable round there?

GERRY. 'Is it safe?' Are the streets of London safe?

FELIX *considers. An announcement interrupts them.*

In England

LARA, ANTON *and* LEYLA *stand surrounded by strings of unintelligible letters. Signposts, headlines, names of shops and institutions, all gibberish.*

Dry Cleaning, Food & Wine, Cheap Calls, To Let, Iceland, Tandoori, Chinese Hot Meals, Internet, Easy Top-Up, Tasty Kebab, Healthcare Centre – all letters out of sequence.

They absorb their surroundings, excited, curious.

They are overwhelmed by information conveyed to them in different local and regional British accents.

– 'You will need to fill this in so we can get you proper representation.'

– 'Do you need an interpreter?'

– 'Where did you come from?'

– 'Now, love, look here, we'll need an NI, won't we, otherwise we'll hardly make any headway, alright? NI. National Insurance number.'

– 'What I need from you is two proofs of address… such as utility bills – '

– 'Have you got your Oyster, sweetheart?'

– 'Thank you for calling Citizens Advice Bureau. We are currently experiencing a high volume of calls…'

– 'Thank you for calling Homes and Communities Agency. All our operators are currently unavailable. You have been placed in a queue…'

LARA. They are so polite, aren't they? That is nice. It's nice that people are kind to each other. If they accidentally push you getting on the bus or step on your toes, they will apologise. Whereas at home, if you don't use your elbows you'll be stuck on the bus for ever.

ANTON. The city is big. It doesn't make sense that anything should be this big.

LEYLA. It feels like the whole planet is in the streets of London.

Interviews II

WOMAN. It's not coming up with your name.

ANTON. I'm sorry?

WOMAN. The computer. It's not coming up with a match for your name.

Silence.

Would you happen to have your reference number with you?

ANTON *struggles to understand.*

ANTON. What?

WOMAN. Reference number. A number? Did you take down the number? When you fill in the application online, you receive a reference number.

ANTON. Erm… what?

WOMAN. The app… Did you fill in the form online? On the computer?

ANTON. No.

WOMAN. No. Well, you might have said so in the first place. Would have saved us a heck of a lot of time, don't you agree?

ANTON. Yes.

WOMAN. Mhm. Let's see then…

She mumbles to herself as she types ANTON*'s details.*

There is very little at the moment, some factory work up in Liverpool.

ANTON. I am carpenter.

WOMAN. Oh, how lovely. So there is an abattoir in Essex, that's not that far away from here in fact. And then there is also the brewery in Dewsbury.

ANTON. A brew…?

WOMAN. Brewery… where they make beer. In Dewsbury. Up north.

ANTON. I like to work out.

WOMAN. Do you?

ANTON. Out in the air.

WOMAN. Oh. Oh, yes, I see. I'm afraid it doesn't work like that, you know… Oh, hang on… here we go. I do have something which allows you plenty of fresh air.

*

SERA *sits in an interview at the Home Office. She is accompanied by a woman* INTERPRETER. *The* INTERPRETER *repeats* SERA's *words in English.* SERA *is timid, reluctant to reply.*

SERA. Yes, I have been given temporary papers. The papers that I left with, originally left with, that is the first time I fled, they were not my real papers. They were fake. Because they wouldn't allow me to cross the border otherwise. I don't have my original papers. I never had any. I never… travelled. I didn't need… I'm telling the truth.

Pause.

They found me in the bushes. I can't remember how I got there.

INTERVIEWER. You don't remember how you got there?

SERA. No.

INTERVIEWER. The country you claim to be your country of origin is not the same country as the country of departure.

SERA *stares at the* INTERVIEWER.

And you would have crossed at least two borders from the country of origin.

SERA. Yes.

INTERVIEWER. But you don't remember crossing those borders.

SERA. ... No. (*Pause.*) I... I see pictures... but I... don't know how to... A man helped me. I think he carried me. I... don't remember.

The INTERVIEWER *shakes her head. She's not convinced.*

I am telling the truth.

Pause.

I just want to find my husband. You will see then...

INTERVIEWER. The telephone number you've supplied is not in use. Your husband's name is not in any of our records.

SERA *stares at the* INTERVIEWER, *struggling to understand.*

If he's here without the proper authorisation, by which I mean, illegally...

SERA. He is not illegal. He said he asked for asylum and was granted. He said it was quick and the people were very nice.

INTERVIEWER. Did he instruct you to ask for asylum?

SERA *is silent. She is unsure of how to reply.*

SERA. If you could just let me find him?

INTERVIEWER. Do you have an address?

SERA. No! I have the number!!

INTERVIEWER. The number is invalid.

SERA. I will go find him?

INTERVIEWER. How do you intend to do that?

SERA. Ask! Ask the people. Go outside... search... ask...

She trails off, frustrated. She starts to cry.

Floor 16. Both Sides of the Glass.

We are on the sixteenth floor of a tall, glass office building.

FELIX *is taking a meeting with Romanian business partners.* GERRY *is present.* ANTON *is also present, in a manner of speaking – from the outside. Strapped in, 'hanging' from the window he is washing, unacknowledged by the others.*

Pictures of wind turbines are displayed around the room.

An animated conversation has been going on for a while.

GERRY. Gentlemen, at the moment our two companies have nine gigawatts of capacity under development. I assure you all the concerns you have we have dealt with before.

> FELIX *gets up and 'takes the stage'.*

FELIX. Mr Gabor, Mr Iliescu, I want you to try and grasp the magnitude of this enterprise. Let's look past all the challenges. Ever since the beginning of time, the planet has been wrapped in, enveloped in a layer of invisible energy. Since the dawn of man and before, this force has been here, existing side by side with us, working for or against us. Look, look outside. What do you see? If we were to open the window, here on the sixteenth floor, you would be surprised at the force with which the elements would immediately hit us. It...

> *He suddenly comes face to face with* ANTON.

... looks like... empty space out there, but in fact it's... it's... an endless pool of resources.

> *He stops for a moment, distracted. He gazes at* ANTON. ANTON *gazes back at him.*

GERRY. Felix?

> FELIX *snaps out.*

FELIX. Yes... We... We only ever managed to put it to use in small, isolated attempts. Like windmills and sailing boats. And we have so far never really managed to see the big picture. How, if you connect the dots, this force turns into energy, this energy is everywhere around us, it has no beginning and no end. It has no bottom to hit, it can not dry up. We are changing the way the planet operates. Make no mistake – we are changing the world. (*Pause.*) Changing the world doesn't happen without resistance. But that should not discourage us. Don't you agree?

Beat.

MR GABOR *extends his hand to* FELIX. *Some champagne bottles pop. A round of congratulations, laughter, patting of backs, shaking of hands.*

Distracted in all of this, FELIX *can't help glancing back at the now-empty window where* ANTON *stood a minute ago.*

Stuff

A small, shabby council house shared between a bunch of people.

LARA *has got a big plastic bag full of items she is taking out and looking over. Her flatmate,* LEYLA, *is looking at the things with her. They both seem excited about it.*

ANTON *is by the side. Sitting. Smoking.*

ANTON. What is that?

LARA. This lady I work for, she gave me some things.

ANTON. What things?

LARA. A couple of mugs. Some hair products.

LEYLA. Why are they so small?

LARA. They're travel-size.

LEYLA. Oh!

ANTON. Because you travel a lot.

LARA *ignores him, clearly excited about the small-sized bottles.*

LARA. A soap dish.

ANTON. A what?

LARA. To keep the soap in.

ANTON. Right. We need something to keep the soap in?

Beat.

LARA. We need… We need things to make this place feel more like… a home.

ANTON. It's not home.

LARA. I didn't say 'like home', I said 'like a home'.

She produces a box.

LEYLA. What's that?

LARA. It's a… chocolate fondue set.

ANTON. A what?

LEYLA. Chocolate fon…

LARA. Fondue.

ANTON *looks at* LARA, *expecting more information.*

It's… It's something to do with cheese. And chocolate. It's for when you have guests. She had a spare set.

ANTON. So… crap she doesn't want any more she gives to you. You're like a little magpie, you can't resist shiny things.

LARA. It's not crap.

ANTON. Where's your pride?

LARA. You know what, Anton? You don't have to use it. You can use paper cups, as a matter of fact. You can dry your hands on your shirt. And you certainly don't have to use the fon– (*Struggles to pronounce it.*) Leave me alone.

She gets up and leaves. LEYLA *follows her.*

Left on his own, ANTON *picks up the fondue set and inspects it.*

Sera's Phone Call

SERA. Erez? Hello? Erez is there?

VOICE. Who?

SERA. Erez. My name Sera. Erez?

VOICE. Who d'you want to speak to?

SERA. Erez. I have number. I want Erez?

VOICE. There's no Erez here, love.

SERA. I have this number.

VOICE. You've got the wrong number.

The line is cut off.

SERA *stares at the number on a piece of paper. She tries to make out the numbers.*

SERA. Three. Could be five.

She dials again. The high-pitched sound of dialling a non-existent line is heard.

Felix Wants a Baby

Late at night, at their long, long kitchen table. ANN *pours sparkling water into their glasses.* FELIX *pulls her closer, he tries to kiss her.*

ANN. No... Felix...

FELIX. 'No, Felix'... I'll have a shirt printed for you. 'No, Felix.'

ANN. I'm sorry. I'm just not in the mood.

FELIX. Are you sure? It might be fun. It's been so long, it might feel like sleeping with an entirely new guy.

ANN. Very funny.

FELIX. Is this new?

ANN. Yes, Felix. The table is new. It is twice the size of the old table.

FELIX. Well, that's what I said. When did we get a new table?

ANN. Today.

FELIX. Oh. Very nice. Why did we get a new table?

ANN. I figured we could use one a bit bigger. It seems right for the space.

FELIX. And the lifestyle. All the kids and the relatives always dropping by.

ANN. Indeed.

He pulls her closer again and starts to kiss her.

FELIX. Come on. The table deserves christening.

She gives in reluctantly.

ANN. Have you got a condom?

FELIX. A condom? What are we, on a blind date?

ANN. No, it's just, I'm off the pill and I'm ovulating.

FELIX. You're off the pill? Since when?

ANN. A little while ago. You were away as usual. It is poison, in fact. I feel like a fraud. Teaching people how to eat and all the while… Ah, never mind.

He fondles her.

FELIX. So, I'll pull out. I'm not seventeen.

She pushes him away.

ANN. I don't want to risk it.

FELIX. Because it would be such a fucking disaster to get pregnant?!

ANN. Felix… we've talked about this before.

FELIX. Let's talk about it again.

ANN. I'm not ready to have a baby.

FELIX. You're thirty-four.

ANN. What's that supposed to mean?

FELIX. It means it's time! We're ready. We can afford it, we have the means, we're married, we're at the right age –

ANN. No, you can afford it. I can't afford it. My business is very fragile. You know very well how precarious the climate is at the moment, I have to be a hundred per cent committed. And when we have a baby, nothing changes for you, you go on as before. Everything changes for me. My life goes on hold!

FELIX. Having a baby means your life goes on hold?

ANN. I'm not ready!

FELIX. Fine! Fine. Let's not have a baby. Let's not even fuck any more until you're ready. How's that?

ANN. Ah, Felix…

He imitates the expression on her face as she says 'Ah, Felix.' He starts opening a bottle of wine.

I thought we were –

FELIX. We're not any more.

He puts two wine glasses on the table and pours himself a large glass. She covers the other glass with her hand. He drinks his wine.

ANN. What is this urge to get pregnant?

FELIX. I don't know.

ANN. You've got a massive project on your hands –

FELIX (*agitated*). Yes, I know –

ANN. Aren't you excited?

FELIX. Yes, sure. I'm excited. I just thought… It'd be nice –

His hands go up as if holding a football.

Something... actual... human-size... solid – I mean... I don't know.

ANN *observes him. She can't make out what is going on in his head. Or maybe she can, but she chooses not to. Not right now. Later.*

ANN. I need to do some work.

FELIX. Sure. So do I.

They both start tapping away at their laptops.

Don't you ever feel – regardless of the circumstances – don't you sometimes feel a desire – when you're out in the street walking with your arms dangling, a desire to know what it feels like when a small hand reaches up and takes yours? A small child who trusts you implicitly with his hand nesting in yours, letting you lead him through the world?

ANN. When do you ever find time to walk around, 'arms dangling', lost in abstract thought, if I might ask?

Silence.

I mean... Of course I wonder.

She looks at him. She goes back to the laptop.

The sound of tapping fills the space.

Lara and the Sewing Kit

ANTON *sits smoking a cigarette.*

LARA *stands next to him, like a teacher.*

ANTON. You go. I'll stay.

LARA. Come on.

ANTON. I'm too tired.

LARA. It's important. It's important we learn the language.

ANTON. We get by.

LARA. That's not enough.

ANTON. I don't need to speak perfect English to wash the
windows.

LARA. You'll get a better job if you speak better English. You
know it's important. I'm not staying in this dump for ever.

Silence.

I'll go to school and get a job and... you know... one day I'll
get a nice house and who knows... I'll meet a nice man.

ANTON. Sure.

LARA. And so will you. Meet a woman. Have a family. Things
will happen.

Silence.

I have talents, you know. I can sew. I can make clothes. I
could... design clothes.

ANTON. Yeah, that's what they've been waiting for here. You
with your sewing kit.

LARA. You can be such an arsehole.

Silence.

ANTON. I'm sorry. I'm tired. And cold. Come here.

*He pulls her closer. He tries to kiss her. She kisses him back
but pulls away.*

LARA. No... not now. I have to go. You should come. Why is it
so cold?

ANTON. I don't know.

LARA. Did you put the money in the meter? It was your turn.

ANTON. I know it was my turn. I did.

LARA. Then why is it so cold?

ANTON. I don't know.

She storms out. She comes back angry.

LARA. You didn't do it right. Why didn't you do it right? It used up the emergency credit and then it locked itself. We have to call somebody. Why didn't you do it properly?

ANTON. I thought I did.

LARA. I showed you how to do it. It's not that difficult.

ANTON. I thought I did! Give me a break! It's fucking confusing. What kind of a stupid system is that? I never heard of anything so stupid and humiliating in my whole life. A meter? Is it World War II? Are we imbeciles? Can we not be trusted with normal bills!

He punches the wall in frustration.

LARA *is silent.*

I'm sorry.

Silence.

LARA *takes out the* Yellow Pages. *She looks through. She dials.*

LARA. Hello? Hello. This is Lara speaking. I have your number from *Yellow Pages*. Hi. I have problem with... meter. Meter for boiler... Excuse me?...

She looks like she's in pain.

I don't understand... Can you tell me how much it costs? ... Excuse me?...

She hangs up.

ANTON. What? What?

LARA. I can't talk to him. I don't understand anything. He talks like he has a hot potato in his mouth.

ANTON. How much did he say?

LARA. Seventy pounds per hour.

They both go silent. ANTON *puts his jacket on.*

Where are you going?

ANTON. I'll go to the pub. One of our guys must know something about boilers.

LARA. Oh. Yes, that's a good idea.

ANTON. What about your class?

He lingers, feeling guilty.

LARA. I'm late.

ANTON. Do you want something?

LARA. No. Thank you.

ANTON *looks at her for a moment, then leaves.*

She puts some more clothes on. She turns the television on and stares at it. The blue television light glows in her face.

Interviews III

LARA *is cleaning a kitchen in a well-off household. She turns a lamp to shine directly in her face. A little like an interrogation light. Or indeed a camera light. She lets go of the cloth and assumes an air of ownership.*

LARA. Would you like a cup of tea? Milk and sugar? I take it quite strong. You know, before I came here I couldn't imagine putting milk in tea. And now I can't get enough of it. (*Pause.*) Yes, it was tough the first few years. Very tough. But even when it was very hard... you learn things every day. Every day you are a little better at... living here. I can't explain. First time I had *A to Z* in my hands, I wanted to cry. Then one day you just catch yourself going '5C, eighty-nine.' (*Pause as if to hear a question.*) I worked as a cleaner. I don't say that I was a cleaner, I just worked as a cleaner. I'm not ashamed of cleaning. You have to make money. I was a good cleaner because I clean houses like they were my own. And we are much more thorough with cleaning than English. Yes, I have a cleaner now. I treat her well. I'm not saying she's my best friend but I take an interest. I never behave like she is not there. (*Pause.*) Well, this is how it happened. One lady I worked for, she was going to throw out some of her clothes. I asked if I could have them. They were very fine, expensive clothes. Then I went home and I changed them to fit me. I also changed the design a bit. When she saw what I did, she was impressed. She recommended me to a friend who had a company that makes clothes. So I started to work for him and slowly, little by little I started my own business, making clothes. It's doing very well now. Karen, that's the lady I worked for, she and I are good friends now. She even wears the clothes I make now.

*

ANTON *sits at the kitchen table. In front of him is a stack of old newspapers. He picks up a copy of the* Daily Mail. *He concentrates on a story and tries to read out loud in a flat tone, struggling through the sentences.*

ANTON. 'Meet the incredible shrinking mother who lost half her body weight by shedding eleven stone in just nine months.' Shrinking mother…

He ponders. He frowns, unable to make sense of it. Agitated, he turns a few pages.

Now *that's* travelling in style! Illegal immigrants 'smuggled into New York on world's most luxurious cruise liner'.

He stops to think. He flicks through more pages.

Weather. 'Tsunami terror for British holidaymakers.'

He gives up. He pushes the newspapers away.

He picks them up again. He goes through the pages and settles on a story and begins to focus.

The Coffee Experience

FELIX *is in a café, working on his laptop.* CUSTOMERS *are lined up in front of a big window, with headphones in their ears, staring at their screens. The sound of tapping pervades the space.*

A waitress (LEYLA) *brings* FELIX *a coffee. She startles him as she puts the cup on his table. He mouths a 'thank you'.*

In the background, two GIRLS *have entered the café. They take their seats at an empty table and begin to chat. Their conversation is unclear but it is certainly the sound of two human voices.*

They interfere with FELIX*'s concentration. He starts getting impatient, throwing them angry looks. The* GIRLS *soon begin to chuckle. The chuckling becomes louder and louder, distorted in* FELIX*'s mind.*

He slams his fist on the table. The coffee cup tumbles down on the floor. The chuckling abruptly stops, the GIRLS *and all the other* CUSTOMERS *look up at* FELIX, *puzzled, taken aback.*

FELIX   Would you mind? Would you fucking mind?!

> FELIX *stops, suddenly self-conscious and embarrassed. The* GIRLS *stare at him in shock. He looks dazed.* LEYLA *comes over to clean up the spilt coffee.*

> I'm sorry. I'm so sorry. Let me help you with this.

LEYLA. It's okay. I can.

FELIX. No, please, how clumsy of me. I really am awfully sorry.

LEYLA. It's okay.

Lara Gets a Kitchen Table

LARA *stands in front of a kitchen table, outside her house.*

Two young boys approach.

BOY 1. Hey. Oi. You.

> LARA *looks at him. She doesn't respond.*

BOY 2. Can't get it through the door?

LARA. No.

BOY 1. Door not wide enough, huh?

LARA. No, I just…

BOY 2. Don't you have doors where you come from, eh? D'you not know how to use a door?

LARA. I'm okay…

BOY 1. Do you live in a fucking tent?

BOY 2. Okay, tell you what, if we help you get this through the door, what you gonna do for us?

LARA. No, I… Thank you, I don't need help.

> *She climbs up on the table.*

BOY 1. How 'bout we do a deal? We get your table through the door and you give us a blowjob. How's that? I reckon that sounds fair.

LARA. Please, leave me alone.

BOY 2. Too late, sweetheart –

> *They start spinning the table.* LARA *feels increasingly alarmed as the* BOYS *laugh and cheer.*

> ANTON *appears. He takes one of the* BOYS *by the jacket and throws him to the floor.*

BOY 1. Hey!

ANTON. Leave her alone.

BOY 2 runs up to ANTON, *but* ANTON *is clearly bigger than him.* BOY 1 *gets up.*

BOY 2. Get your filthy hands off me, fucking scum!

BOY 1. Why don't you fuck off where you came from?

BOY 2. Like I'd touch her? I wouldn't be seen dead touching her. Catch fucking AIDS off her or something.

BOY 1. Bird flu.

They start to laugh.

BOY 2. Bird flu! Swine flu!

BOY 1. Stab him!

BOY 2. I know where you live, cunt. You're dead.

They run off.

ANTON. You okay?

LARA. Yes.

He comes closer. He strokes her face. He wants to put his arm around her, but she pulls back.

I'm fine.

Pause.

Thanks.

He shrugs.

ANTON. What's this?

LARA. It's a kitchen table.

ANTON. I see that.

LARA. It's from this new woman I just started to work for.

ANTON. You just started to work for her and already she's giving you her old crap. You strike gold every time.

But he has a smile on his face.

LARA. It's not crap. It's a good, expensive table.

He strokes the wood with the touch of an expert.

ANTON. So it is. Actually. Very good. Solid wood.

LARA. See. I can get good stuff.

Silence.

ANTON. I don't think it will fit in our kitchen.

LARA. I know.

She starts to whimper.

It's so stupid. She said, 'Take it if you like.' I could see it wouldn't fit. But I thought – a nice, good-quality table that looks like it belongs in a nice, happy house. Where people sit around it and talk and hot food is served. I don't want to be like them, eat off our laps, stare at the telly. Come home tired, exhausted, crash in silence… It was a stupid thing to do.

She sighs.

ANTON. No. You did well to get the table.

She looks at him surprised.

Very… resourceful. I… will have a look. I can probably refit it so we can squeeze it in the kitchen.

LARA. Really?

ANTON. Of course. I wasn't always a window cleaner, you know.

She smiles. She kisses him. They kiss.

Dinner Party

FELIX, ANN, GEORGE *and* LOUISE *sit at the long, long kitchen table. A tall vase with three white flowers in the centre.*

GEORGE. So we thought, why not? I mean, America is, after all, the promised land.

LOUISE. With a few bumpy roads.

GEORGE. Plenty. Still, ultimately, it is. Don't get me wrong, there are a lot of lucrative areas in Europe, most of which you have already tapped into –

He looks at FELIX *and gives a knowing smirk.* FELIX *doesn't acknowledge it.*

But for my money… They are somehow more – they think on a grand scale. Maybe that's to do with how vast the country is, you know, open views, wide roads. There is no space here. I'm starting to feel claustrophobic.

ANN. So, you're leaving.

LOUISE. In October.

ANN. Well…

LOUISE. It makes sense, really. George spends more time on a plane than he does at home. In fact, sometimes I get a distinct feeling that he's mistaken me for a stewardess.

They laugh. FELIX *sort of laughs.*

ANN. I'll miss you.

LOUISE. Oh. You'll come out though. Any time. It'd be so lovely to have you.

ANN. I'd love to. But I can't see how… with my business just starting out –

LOUISE. Well, you should come on a research trip. Explore the market. I mean, if they like nutritionists anywhere, it's in America. Right, George? Think globally!

FELIX. Why do we say – 'come out'?

LOUISE. Pardon?

FELIX. 'Come out.' Come out to LA, come out to New York. What's that about? As if there was a link, some path that spontaneously takes us from here to America. We're here, gnawing at our sorry claustrophobic existence and then if things go well we 'come out' to America.

Silence.

GEORGE. I'm sorry, Felix, Louise didn't mean...

He exchanges looks with ANN *and his wife.*

Well, I certainly didn't mean to imply –

ANN. It's alright, George.

FELIX. No, no. No, it's not you. It's the concept. I'm just... talking about the concept.

An uncomfortable silence.

Obviously, it'll be fantastic for you. A new world. You see, I sometimes think it's not natural to move around that much. You know – roots and that sort of thing. But actually, those are only fleeting reactionary moments. People have been in migration since the dawn of man, haven't they?

GEORGE. Yes. Well, yes, exactly. My great-grandmother was French. Her family came over with the Huguenots. You know, the silk-weavers. I like to think that's where I get my sense of style.

LOUISE. Yes. And the aroma of cheese that often lingers around you.

They laugh.

GEORGE. Louise's grandfather was Hungarian.

ANN. I've recently discovered that my ancestors, now this was a very long time ago, but they seem to have come from Sudan. Isn't that bizarre?

FELIX. I'm thinking, we could move.

Pause.

ANN (*stunned*). I'm sorry?

FELIX. We could go live somewhere else.

ANN. Like where?

FELIX. Romania. Or Serbia. I hear it's great fun.

ANN. Have you lost your mind?

FELIX. Why? You were just saying, people migrate. They have done since… like a hundred thousand years ago…

ANN. Yes, in search of better, not worse.

FELIX. You don't know it would be going for the worse. We'd be on a good salary. New lifestyle, new experiences. Making an actual difference in a society. It would be good for business if I was there. This guy I work with, Gerry, is now based in Romania – he says it's a blast.

Pause as they look at each other.

ANN. Are you saying that you have to move?

FELIX. No! No. What the fuck, Ann. I'm not… It's not an ambush. I'm just saying, it's an option. It's not like we have a child.

ANN rolls her eyes.

ANN. Felix has decided that he wants a baby. Right now.

LOUISE. Oh. Well. That's… erm… We have been thinking about it as well.

GEORGE. We'd love to.

LOUISE. It's just not the right time.

ANN. Exactly.

LOUISE. With the move –

ANN. Of course –

GEORGE. Surely, with your projects in Eastern Europe, it's not the right time?

FELIX. To move to Eastern Europe?

ANN. What about my job? What about my practice – I can't just pick up and –

FELIX. Why not? You think they don't want nutritionists over there? They're gagging for them. You'll be a guru. They'll build you a temple. You'll have kudos coming out of your arse!

ANN. I don't want kudos behind the fucking Iron Curtain. I want kudos here.

She stops. Silence.

LOUISE. I think George was referring to the baby.

Pause.

FELIX. No, you're right. It's not the right time. I just… Don't you feel like a baby gives a sense of purpose to one's life?

ANN. You don't bring another human being into the world for you. Besides, your job has a purpose.

FELIX. What's its purpose?

ANN. Saving the planet.

FELIX. That's not the purpose of my job. Making money is the purpose of my job. A bunch of people in this world are smart enough to understand that there is no infinite flow of profit where the resources are drying up. Furthermore, that investing in renewable energy is in fact a more lucrative course of action. That's what my job is actually about. Saving the planet is just a blurb.

LOUISE. George –

GEORGE. That's awfully cynical, mate. Whether people are making money on it or not, it is still doing the planet a lot of good (save for a few birds you knock off on the way, but no more than your average English aristocrat in the course of a year), and you are changing the way the planet operates. So, it's hardly a meaningless feat –

ANN. Thank you.

FELIX *considers.*

FELIX. I yelled at some girls in a café.

ANN. What?

FELIX. I was working. At the computer.

In fact, dealing with the results of a post-mortem performed on a bunch of dead Romanian birds which were thought to have been killed by wind turbines but had in fact gorged on grapes, leftover from the wine-making process. In other words, they drank themselves to death.

ANN. Felix, what –

FELIX. Two girls came in and started chatting and giggling and... and... I lost it. I exploded, I knocked my coffee over, I went over to their table and yelled at them to keep quiet. In the middle of a café, because human voices were interfering with my work.

Silence.

Our ambition is to change the way the planet functions. And if that wasn't enough, the ambition is always to be the first one to do it. I don't know how to rewind to a place where ambitions were smaller and I was happy about it. This idea of everything being global is a mind-fuck! I don't think my brain can handle 'global'!

ANN, LOUISE *and* GEORGE *are silent, unsure of how to respond.*

I mean, don't you sometimes feel like your seams are going to give?

GEORGE. Well, Felix, everyone feels like that sometimes. We're all under tremendous pressure – that's just the life nowadays.

FELIX. No. No. That's wrong. We go about it as though... as though... it's something one simply gets on with. You know... and... when you ask yourself, you know... What's it really about? What do we really need? What really makes you happy? Why are you moving to America? You think it's going to make you happy? You think that somehow, you move away and become different people? Or the people you used to be? The people that have fun and enjoy life. You think you'll have more sex? Do you even want to have sex with each other any more? I mean, we're all 'going global', we want more and more of everything, we change our phones every five minutes because a newer shinier version comes out but we're sticking to the one partner? We don't want anything different? And if we are, if that's the case, why the hell do our partners detest us so much? You know? Do you… Or is it just me…

Silence.

ANN. Thank you, Felix. Well, I'm sure that… erm…

Silence.

LOUISE. Maybe a… a nice, long holiday…

Her words fall dead in the awkward silence.

News from Home

Noise of a busy London street. ANTON *stands, waiting.*

STEFAN *arrives. Both men are shocked to see each other.*

ANTON. Stefan?

STEFAN. Brother?

ANTON. You're the guy I'm meeting?

STEFAN *opens his arms – here he is.*

A guy at the pub said he knew a guy who knew a guy who's the guy to go to.

STEFAN *nods.*

That's you?

STEFAN. What can I tell you, brother? Information is everything.

ANTON *laughs.*

How are you? I looked for you.

ANTON. So you don't know everything.

STEFAN. And you like to lay low.

Pause.

But you made it. How are you?

ANTON. I'm alright. You?

STEFAN. Good. Good. You know. Good.

ANTON. Work?

STEFAN. A hotel for a while. Fucking dreadful. I'm at the door of that club 'The Vault'?

No reaction on ANTON'*s face.* STEFAN *laughs.*

Of course. You don't know about it. Well, that will change. You'll come. I can get you in. Which is not easy.

ANTON. Okay, brother. I'll come to see your Vault. Lara would like that, I'm sure.

STEFAN. Oh, Lara.

He says that with much significance, which ANTON *sympathetically ignores.*

ANTON. So, it's a good job?

STEFAN. Well, you see things, you hear things, you get to know people. And you know what I say –

ANTON. Information is everything.

They laugh.

STEFAN. What do you need?

ANTON. … You don't have any news from home, do you?

STEFAN. No, not for a while.

ANTON. About my father? You didn't hear anything.

STEFAN. No, I'm sorry, man. I don't know.

ANTON. And the nuns?

Beat.

The nuns. In the convent?

STEFAN. You don't know?

Pause.

ANTON. No. What?

STEFAN *checks his watch. He looks around, uncomfortable.*

STEFAN. They went through the town, I suppose I don't have to tell you about that. Momo was the lead. (*Pause.*) It's the location of the convent – up in the hills, cut into the rock. Good views, protected from the back. (*Pause.*) They set up camp there. They stayed a couple of months.

ANTON. Did they kill them?

STEFAN. No. They didn't kill them. (*Pause.*) After they left, the four younger ones… were all pregnant.

ANTON *listens, tense.*

They… they all committed suicide, Anton.

Beat.

The rest of them won't say what exactly went on…

Pause.

ANTON. Suicide is eternal damnation.

STEFAN. Well, I don't believe that –

ANTON. But they did.

STEFAN. Yes.

Silence amid the sounds of a busy London street, amid other people's lives passing them by.

I'm sorry.

STEFAN *squeezes* ANTON's *shoulder.* ANTON *sits down on the pavement.* STEFAN *sits down next to him.*

Sera's Phone Call

SERA. Erez? Hello? Erez is there?

VOICE. Who?

SERA. Erez. My name Sera. Erez?

VOICE. Who d'you want to speak to?

SERA. Erez.

VOICE. There's no Erez here, love.

SERA. I have this number.

VOICE. You've got the wrong number.

The line is cut off.

SERA *stares at the number on a piece of paper.*

Anchor and Hope

ANTON *and* STEFAN *sit at a table in a pub.*

ANTON. She's got a kitchen table. She brings things into the house. She is trying to make it pleasant. I mostly grumble. I can't help it. I don't like it here. And I don't want to learn to like it. I don't want to do my best to make it nice and then… What if…

STEFAN. She's right. There is a lot of life left to be lived.

ANTON. Too much.

STEFAN. It's easier if you have someone to share it with. If she wants to be with you –

ANTON. She doesn't want to be with me. I am like a waiting room. With pots of flowers. She cares, I know. But she wants a future. I'm not a man with a future.

Pause.

STEFAN. I used to think I was going to be somebody.

Pause.

Let's get another drink.

ANTON. I was somebody. Not a very important person. But I had a job I liked. I was left in peace to do it. People respected it. I went about my business, I had some good friends. Didn't get on with my sister – I'm not on good terms with God. Most of my life, didn't get on with my father. I suppose no son does. Last few years, we lived together in… what you might call harmony. (*Pause.*) I wanted to marry once. And then her father gambled her away. Yeah. Literally. Lost her to a guy I went to school with. You wouldn't think that sort of thing happens nowadays. She was too timid to stand up to him. He was a bully. Gave her away to a bully. A bully by the name of Dane. (*Pause.*) Anyway. (*Pause.*) It's not a bad job, washing windows. Carpentry is better. Carpentry is bringing things to people. Things they'll live with. I wash windows and watch people live. I try not to. But I can't help it. There was a woman crying today. In her flat. She let us in, she tried to control herself, but she couldn't. She went into the bathroom and I could hear her sobbing. All the time we were there. Most people just go about their business as though we weren't there. They have telephone conversations, with their wives, with their lovers, with their psychiatrists… Some are very nice to us, but, I suppose, where would it get them, if they tried to acknowledge everyone, all the cleaners, all the staff. (*Pause.*) We were doing a building in the City the other day. I was up on the sixteenth floor. I thought, if I unhooked my belt, if I let the wind knock me over, if I fell, if I hit the pavement like a pancake, would these people in this meeting notice? Would they rush down to the street? Would anyone ask what my name was? Would anyone miss me? I've no one left to miss me. Lara, maybe. For a while.

Silence.

Do you feel like you're in a dream? Do you feel like it's not even your dream? Someone else's crazy subconscious is making the decisions.

Interviews IV

At the US Embassy, LOUISE *arrives for her visa interview.*

She puts her belongings in a tray. She opens her bag for inspection.

GUARD. Ma'am, is that a cellphone?

LOUISE. Yes, but it's switched off.

GUARD. You have been advised to leave all your electronic devices, such as a cellphone or a car key, outside of these premises. We can not allow you to proceed with the interview if you are still in possession of these items.

LOUISE. Oh… Oh. Erm… I thought I was not allowed to use the mobile… the cellphone, which is why it is switched off.

GUARD. You are not allowed to enter the building with a cellphone or any other electronic or battery-operated equipment.

LOUISE. Oh. Oh, I see! You mean because of the…

She mimics an explosion. The GUARD *doesn't so much as move a muscle.*

Yes, of course. Erm… well, shall I… Would you like me to… Is there a safety deposit box?

GUARD. No, ma'am.

LOUISE. Right. Well, you see, my problem is this – I could pop to the car and leave my phone there. That's not a problem. But I would then have to lock the car with the key which I would then have nowhere to deposit, are you with me?

The GUARD *shrugs.*

You know… you're… I must say, with all due respect, you are being rather unhelpful. Erm… if I'm honest.

*

Later, during the interview, LOUISE *fidgets sitting on a chair. The* INTERVIEWER *sits across from her.*

INTERVIEWER. Have you had a criminal conviction in any country incl–

LOUISE. No.

INTERVIEWER. Including traffic offences?

LOUISE. Oh. Erm… No. (*Pause.*) Well…

The INTERVIEWER *looks up.*

I've gone through a red light. Several times. In several countries. I'm not sure if that's the sort of thing you meant but I thought better to be frank, right?

The INTERVIEWER *holds her gaze and then slowly looks back down at the papers. He takes his time.*

I don't mean to rush you… erm… but you see, I left my car unlocked… erm… so I'm a bit nervous…

She realises this is not going to make an impression on the stone-faced INTERVIEWER, *so she abandons the argument.*

INTERVIEWER. Have you ever been or do you intend to be part of or affiliated with a terrorist organisation?

LOUISE. Erm… Oh. No, I… I … don't think so, no. Heavens.

INTERVIEWER. You don't think so? You're not sure?

LOUISE. No, I… I am sure. I have most certainly never been part of a terrorist organisation.

Pause.

As for affiliation… well, one never knows.

INTERVIEWER. What do you mean?

LOUISE. Well, you hear things, don't you. I mean… stories. Of, you know, phone calls. Say a terrorist accidentally dials a number. It can happen to terrorists as it can to anyone. They misdial. And you pick up. It happens to be your number. Or worse still, you don't pick up. He… or she for that matter, leaves a message. 'This is such and such, Salim Hafiz al… Fayed.' You know. Or he doesn't say his name, he says a code name, 'This is, I don't know, Black Hijab,' I mean, probably not, well, I don't know what their code names are,

in any case he – or maybe he doesn't leave a message, he
probably wouldn't leave a message, he's not daft, is he? But
what happens nevertheless, if he is being monitored, which
he probably is, all Muslims are being monitored I should
think, you have it on your records that he tried to phone me.
Little good will it do me to later try and prove that the Black
Hijab or what's-his-name dialled the wrong number. And
then, say, I don't know, I heard that this happened once,
right. You go to a shop and 'Oh, look at that, black pepper on
sale.' And you think, 'Oh, that'll be nice as I like black
pepper.' And you buy a jumbo pack. And you think, 'While
I'm at it, I might get a packet for Mum.' And boom, two kilos
of ground black pepper along with a funny number in your
phone, that's already grounds for interrogation, am I right?

INTERVIEWER. Mrs Emms, have you received
communication from persons you have reason to suspect are
involved in terrorist activity?

LOUISE. Well, no. Have I not made myself clear? I'm just
saying that should you find any such evidence in my phone
records, that would be pure coincidence.

In Therapy

FELIX. I would look at those turbines and they seemed like
blenders to me. Like I'm stuck in some kind of… dough and
it's revolving really fast and I'm in it right up to my chin and
I can't come out.

He trails off, struggling to find words.

I find it difficult to feel happy. If I'm on my own, I find it
difficult not to sink. Being around other people tends to lift
my spirits. But then, I suspect that might be simply because
I'm too insecure to let them see the real me. The miserable,
gloomy, despairing me. I feel confused a lot of the time as to
what my goal is in life. I can work sixteen hours a day but
then simple tasks, simple obstacles like having to speak to a

phone company or going around roadworks... or Tube delays or... or even struggling to open a bag of nuts can bring me to the verge of tears. I wait for the weekend to have a life and then I can't get it together to get out of bed.

Every... every so often... on a regular basis... I need to remind myself of the good things in life. Health, income, a loving partner, a comfortable home, living in the most exciting city in the world. You tire of London, you tire of life, isn't that how the saying goes? Well... of course I'm not tired, I'm thirty-five. How can I be tired?

So I remind myself how all of this could be gone in a second, I could be diagnosed with some terrible illness tomorrow. Which I'm sure I will be. That makes it even harder. That makes me feel like I really really need to grab these times by the horns... and I feel like... sleeping.

Sometimes I'm happy in my dreams. I remember there was this one dream. I was in a cottage, somewhere that resembled Switzerland. Never-ending green and deep clear water. It was the most beautiful... I can't explain to you how beautiful it was. Maybe that's how beauty feels when you're happy. There was a woman. It wasn't Ann. It was a woman I didn't know and yet she felt familiar. She came up to the porch, she was carrying a bunch of bright wild flowers. And she gave them to me and she said: 'I love you.' I don't think I have ever felt that intensely happy in my whole life as I did in that dream. And in those few seconds when I woke up before it dissolved.

Am I not the most pathetic man?

ANN. He thinks I don't understand him. I do understand him. Every day there is reason to collapse. Sure. Life is disappointing. Friends are selfish, our bodies are unreliable and diminishing in value faster than an average laptop. Pleasure is hard to come by. Falling in love is the only true adrenaline rush worth anything. But falling in love is getting increasingly more difficult with age. The world is infinitely screwed up and you know, at thirty-four, that the next thirty or forty years, if you're lucky, will be more of the same. Probably not even that because we'll get ill at some point. (*Pause.*) The point is – it is a choice to look at life like that,

Felix. If you're not living under a bridge, if you're not in prison, or in a refuge, or homeless or destitute, then it's a choice, and a really fucking spoilt one, to look at life like that. You don't collapse. That's not what one does.

FELIX. Do you think I'm a good man?

THERAPIST. What I think about you is irrelevant.

FELIX. You wouldn't say that if the answer was – yes.

THERAPIST. I would.

FELIX. Well then, that's sad.

A Seventh Man

ANTON *is remodelling the kitchen table. He is focused on work. In his hands, the table is transformed.*

STEFAN. Information travels both ways. What you do when you're away finds a way of reaching the people back home. His father went to work abroad. And then his uncle, following in his brother's footsteps. At that time all migrants had to be examined by a doctor. Those who weren't healthy, didn't get the job. Because their health is not the responsibility of the employer or the country they came to work in. They have no history or age or future. They have one function – to work. All other functions belong to the world they left behind.

The word got back to the village – his uncle was selling urine. His own healthy urine to other less healthy migrants. He's helping them out, he would claim. But he wasn't giving it away. He was selling it. Today they would call him business-minded. Back then he was a disgrace.

People in the village sometimes talked about it at, under the breath but loud enough for Mykola to hear. He never said anything. You can sometimes drink and share the silence with others who have come back. His brother, he knew, would never be back.

The Golden Gherkin

ANTON *is concentrating hard on an article in a glossy magazine.*

LARA. What are you doing?

ANTON. Nothing.

She takes the magazine from him to look at the cover.

LARA. *'Homes and Gardens'*?

ANTON. I found it at work. In the bin. I am learning 'vocabulary'.

He takes the magazine back.

'The – worktop – is – a – key – fe… featur – of Gemma and Toby Crofton-Hewitt's new kitchen – and it took them – nearly – five months – to get – it right.'

LARA *giggles.*

LARA. Well, good for them.

They look through the magazine together. He struggles with pronunciation.

'Deciding on the exact combination of aggregates was a painstaking process and the designer Andrew Getz created ten samples before Toby and Gemma were satisfied.'

She shakes her head in disbelief and starts flicking through the magazine.

Look at that. Can you believe that people live like that? (*Pause.*) You know what I'd like? I'd like to live in one of those houses with bay windows and a little strip of garden in the front. With a fireplace and wooden floors. And when I go out, I'd like to wave to the neighbours across the street.

ANTON. Crofton-Hewitts?

LARA. Go to the market. Remember Borough Market? I'd spend a month's worth of electricity money on a squid. Remember those big ones, the size of a shoe?

ANTON. And stop getting reduced mackerel?

LARA *giggles.*

LARA. And then I could bring my family over. And we could put a Christmas tree in the bay window and –

She stops.

I'm sorry.

Pause.

ANTON. It's alright.

LARA. Do you want to talk about it?

ANTON. No.

He looks at another article.

A perfect dining table.

LARA. You make a better table than any of these. If they knew what hands of gold you had, they'd snap you up in a second.

He smiles.

Huh, I could have some nice fish stew now.

ANTON. Or some beef and cabbage.

LEYLA appears and joins them at the table.

LEYLA. Pomegranate soup. I keep thinking about pomegranate soup.

LARA. And a cup of strong coffee.

ANTON. I can't get used to the tea. Those nice people who offer a cup, always offer tea. Never coffee. I don't know a polite way to say 'I hate tea'… I have tea when I'm sick. What a man needs when he works all day building or washing windows is a stiff drink.

MALIK and STEFAN appear and join the table.

MALIK. Everyone is always saying 'sorry' here. How is that possible? In my country, you say 'sorry' and it's not an easy word to say. If you do something wrong, you admit to it, you say sorry and it means a lot. Here, you hear it all the time and it doesn't mean anything. 'There is nothing we can do for you, sorry.' 'Your case is closed, sorry.' 'I can't help you, sorry.' But nobody is sorry.

LARA. What was the story, Anton? When the man's son went off to the world. Did he happen upon a golden bird? Or was it that he found gold on the ground like his father said.

ANTON. The gold fell from the sky. But it fell from high up so when it hit the ground it went down very deep.

STEFAN. I don't mind digging. I knew there would be digging. I just feel like we keep digging in the wrong place. They know exactly where to dig and we'll never know.

MALIK. People say it will be different. And you think, 'Okay, I am okay with different as long as it's safe.' But the thing with different is – there is no way of knowing how 'different' is going to feel. At home things were bad. But life was a river, it flowed by and I flowed with it. People knew me, their faces lit up when they saw me. Life was a whirlpool and I was in it. Life and I were tied together. And here no one knows me. No one smiles, sometimes they frown. I am grateful for the frown. It makes me feel like I still have flesh. Here life has cut me off. I can see it's there. Other people live it. I see them. Coming out of restaurants, their laughter clanking in the wind, their bodies pleasantly heavy from the food and the alcohol and the warmth. They hail for cabs and kiss and they sink into the seats and off they go. They don't notice me. They step over me as I stand there, observing them, catching their strange scents. I am only a fading figure in the grey landscape of this faraway place.

Silence.

LARA. It's better to regret things you have done than things you haven't done.

MALIK. I had no choice. So I have no regrets.

SERA *appears at the table.*

SERA. This place is near an airport. I can hear planes day and night. Leaving, arriving… People are going places. People can get on a plane and go any place they want. My whole life I have had to look over my shoulder. My whole life I knew danger was never too far away. I fled, once, twice, three times, in the night, in the rain, over the sea, with other people's sweat and breath and blood and faeces all over me. I came to find my husband. We were going to have a decent life. We were going to be happy.

I am in a cell. The door is locked. They don't call it prison. They assure me it's not for ever. But they can't give me a date. Is it a week, a month, a year? They can't say. Until my case is resolved. Not knowing how long is the same as for ever. I wish I could remember what happened. I try so so hard to remember what happened. But I can't. All I can remember are the days far in the past. Meals we had together. My mother's face behind a veil of steam rising from a bowl of rice.

LEYLA *produces a jar of gherkins from the fridge.*

LEYLA. Lara…

LARA. What?

LEYLA. Another one?

LARA. Yes.

LEYLA. And is this one any good?

LARA. It's alright.

LEYLA. Are you going to eat them?

LARA. I don't know. You can have them if you like.

LEYLA. I don't want them. (*Pause.*) I'm throwing them out.

LARA. No!

LEYLA. There is no room for anything else, you've got twelve bloody jars of gherkins in here!

LARA. Don't you shout at me.

LEYLA. Lara, that's… crazy!

LARA. It's not crazy. I can't find the right ones! They just don't taste the same as the ones at home!

ANTON *inspects the jar in question.*

ANTON. Alright, alright! Lara, these look about right.

LARA. Yes, they look right. But they're not. They're too soggy. They are all either too soggy or too spicy, or too sour or… Why is it impossible to find a jar of normal-tasting gherkins? I mean… they're gherkins! They should be the same, like broccoli or, you know, pears!

Pause.

LEYLA. Get rid of them then!

LARA. There's ten pounds' worth of gherkins in there. Ten pounds! I even went to Marks and Spencer and paid £1.69 for one of them. How can I throw it all out? And I can't take them back and I can't give them away and nobody will eat them. It's just fucking depressing.

Pause.

You know what? I am not a refugee. I can always go back if I want to. I am not going to be here at any cost, they are very much mistaken if they think I am.

ANTON. Lara, they don't think about you.

Pause. ANTON *rises from his chair with determination.*

Okay. Bring out the gherkins. We'll eat them now. We'll have a gherkin feast. We'll have a feast of everything we have.

They start to smile, then giggle.

Because where Lara comes from, gherkins are sacred – they give you strength and wisdom, energy and, above all, happiness.

They bring out the jars and more food is put on the table. Spirits are lifted. Drinks are poured.

In fact. That's how the story goes. The wind carried the young man across seven seas and seven hills. He found a town on a hilltop and he thought, 'This looks nice. Maybe here is where I find my happiness.' But when he spoke to the town's chief, the chief said: 'There is no room in our town. The walls have become too tight even for us. You can pitch a tent just outside,

if you like.' But the young man decided to move on. One day
he met a young woman. She was beautiful and alone and
however she tried to pitch her tent in the field, the wind
always blew it away. So the young man took her along.

LARA. She did not have trouble pitching her tent.

ANTON. She had no trouble pitching her tent. Still, she liked
the young man enough to agree to come along with him.

LARA *approves.*

And they came to the land of rain.

At first the man thought, 'What kind of a land is this where
the heaven cries all the time?' But the young woman said –
'Remember, there is nothing worse than drought. Where it
rains, the grass is green and soil is fertile. In this rich land we
shall find our place.' But everywhere they went, it was the
same story all over, no room.

But one night, the darkest of nights, the young man stopped
to drink some water from a river.

He noticed a shining light coming from the bottom of the
river, as shiny as a sunken sun. The young man trod into the
river, reached his hand into the water and pulled out – a
golden gherkin.

They laugh.

LARA. Oh, come on.

ANTON. And it was a talking golden gherkin.

More giggles.

And the gherkin said: 'Don't eat me, I will help you find the
place you're looking for. But first you will have to face three
challenges. One – you have to climb a high, high tower, in
the wind and the rain and bring back a bird feather. Two –
you have to decipher a map of secret routes in a language
unknown. And three –

Pause.

Find a way into the guarded vault. A vault where only the
chosen ones can enter.'

*

GERRY. Ready? I have not been out to London in absolute fucking ages! What's new?

FELIX. I'm afraid, I'm not the right person to ask. I hardly go out.

GERRY. Why is that? You're a good-looking man. Ish. What are you, mid-thirties? Making decent money. Living in London. What's the problem?

FELIX. I'm exhausted, Gerry.

GERRY. That's a sorry state of affairs, mate. We're all exhausted. There are ways to help that –

FELIX. I'm married.

GERRY. Take her along! Send her out with the girls! Buy her loads of shoes that she can stay home and try on.

FELIX. Are you from this century?

*

MALIK. And?

ANTON. We don't know yet. We don't know what secrets are hidden in the vault.

MALIK. I hate secrets.

LEYLA. Anton, and what of the young man's father? Did he send for him?

ANTON. The father had died by then.

LEYLA. No!

STEFAN. Fathers die. And they become the past.

ANTON. But tonight we celebrate their lives. And our lives. And our future.

He embraces LARA.

A Night on the Town

London. Night.

Lights. Traffic.

Noise. Booze.

Glass. Laughter.

Names of bars, clubs, shops, restaurants – now in sequence.

The noise is a recognisable noise of a London street.

GERRY. All I'm saying, mate, is that it's a Friday night.
Everywhere in the world tomorrow is Saturday. Look out
that window – there is a whole, immense, endless,
immeasurable world out there. People, places, women,
pleasure! Don't you want to – dive in?

Just make an unexpected turn somewhere. Into an alley.
Where you haven't been before.

FELIX. That's how you get killed.

GERRY. No, my friend. That's how you live! We'll pretend we
are other people. I'll be Gerhard. From Germany. You can
be... Can you speak any French?

FELIX. A little. I'm fine being English.

GERRY. Okay. You'll be English then. What did you want to be
when you were little?

FELIX *sighs.*

FELIX. An explorer.

GERRY. Well, there you fucking go. Explore. There's a village
for every country in the world in London. Fuck sushi and
cocktails at The Sanderson. Let's go... I don't know... east.

A club. Late at night.

FELIX. 'Let's go east.' It could have been a different side of the
world. He could have said, 'Let's go south.' We could have
gone south. Like the birds.

GERRY. I pity people who stop going to clubs. Too old? What a preposterous notion. The music is too loud? Do you really go to clubs for the music? It's where you go to drink from the fountain of youth.

FELIX. I don't know why, I swear I don't know what came over me, but I took off my wedding ring and I put it in my pocket. Gerry in his obnoxiousness was on to something. Not in the way Gerry thinks of it. 'Take your pick.' Not very likely in my case. But the idea of being in a place like this after such a long time, God, it must have been years, and I was momentarily overwhelmed by a memory of what it was like when all the choice still lay ahead.

ANTON. When she dances she looks like a poster for a world of happy endings.

LARA. She closes her eyes and she is transported somewhere… Where the music goes on for ever.

SERA. A girl in the cell next to me has a transistor radio. She plays music all the time. She says, more than anything else, the silence will kill her. Sometimes I get up and dance. I dance to her music. I close my eyes and I pretend I'm in a crowd of dancing people.

FELIX *and* GERRY *enter the club.* GERRY *goes straight to the bar. Among the people dancing we can make out* LARA. *In fact, if we see it through* FELIX' *eyes, all we can make out is* LARA.

She dances entirely immersed in music, wearing her best clothes, glitter on her smiling face.

ANTON *sits at the bar – as men of that age and background do.*

FELIX. This young woman danced like there was no tomorrow. She was smiling with her eyes closed. She had glitter in her hair and her hips moved in a way that was… hypnotic.

GERRY. That way he moves… I think he believes that to be dancing.

FELIX. My languid limbs actually wanted to join in. What's your name?

LARA. Lara.

FELIX. Lara? What a beautiful name.

LARA. Thank you.

FELIX. Have you seen *Dr Zhivago*?

LARA. Yes. It's long.

FELIX (*laughs*). It is long. Luckily it has Julie Christie in it.
(*Pause.*) Although you're a much more beautiful Lara than her.

He stutters a bit as he compliments her.

LARA *smiles a wide, open, infectious smile.*

LARA. Where are you from?

FELIX. ...Here. I'm from here.

LARA. England?

FELIX. Yes.

LARA. Lucky you.

FELIX. A... aren't you?

LARA. English or lucky?

They laugh.

I'm from Mars!

She swirls as she dances.

But I come in peace.

They laugh as they dance.

As they dance, the music changes. They keep dancing.

SERA. Time is the most unreliable of friends. How it can grind
you down with its relentless length. And how it flies
sometimes, how it slips through your fingers.

FELIX. I did at some point try to explain to her what it is that I
do. The turbines are like giant windmills, you see, and they
produce this energy which is... endless.

LARA. You operate the turbines?

FELIX. No. I mean, in a way, yes.

LARA. So, you are like a miller.

FELIX. A what?

LARA. You bring electricity to the world like millers used to bring flour to the people.

FELIX. Huh, yes… I guess…

LARA. I must tell Anton what we found in the vault!

FELIX. The music was loud, I didn't understand everything she said. But I didn't care. My thoughts had become quite slow. Slow but happy. Somebody said, 'Let's get out of here.' Somebody said something in a language I didn't understand. Gerry said some vaguely embarrassing things in broken Romanian, Serbian and I think a little bit of Japanese… 'I should go home' went through my head for a fleeting second and sank into oblivion.

GERRY. Home is where you go to die.

FELIX. What?

GERRY. What?

FELIX. That's the stupidest thing I've ever heard.

STEFAN. There is something about the last minutes of a night, just before dawn. It tricks you into thinking that whatever happens here and now will disappear with daylight.

GERRY *has got his eye on* LEYLA.

FELIX. Gerry had his eye on a girl, one of Lara's friends who was too drunk to care. And there was the silent guy – strange paternal energy, an X-ray gaze. We were at their house in no time –

GERRY. More drinks…

ANTON. Grown men who can't hold down their drink.

FELIX. You should leave the girl alone. Really, Gerry, she doesn't look in any shape to – But instead he started singing. Lara giggled, I was embarrassed.

LARA. What about you, do you sing?

FELIX. Oh, no. I... Well, I used to. A bit. When I was younger.

LARA. In a band?

FELIX. In a... in a choir...

> LARA *looks at him, she bites her lip to stop herself from laughing. She looks at him, smiling, blinking very slowly.*

> You are very tired.

LARA. Yes. (*Pause.*) I think I have to sleep.

FELIX. My thoughts, my insane thoughts of... my life and ... taking her away...

GERRY. You're the kind of man who never goes after what he wants.

FELIX. He said, salivating over the girl who was all but unconscious. The sight of that girl kept bringing me back to earth. But why not just do what I want to do and worry later? She's still standing there. Looking at me with her big inviting eyes. The silent guy was still there, I could sense his eyes piercing holes in my back.

LARA. Do you... want to... stay?

> *Pause.*

FELIX. I could see him wince. Whose conscience does he think he is? Yes, I wanted to stay. Yes! I wanted to stay! And he would do better to take care of Gerry and the poor girl he was feeling up, who, quite frankly, looked dead from where I was standing.

> You should go to bed.

LARA. Are you sure?

> *Pause.*

FELIX. Yes.

> *Pause.*

LARA. Goodnight.

FELIX (*hurriedly*). Can I call you?

LARA. Yes.

FELIX *smiles, embarrassed, relieved.*

FELIX. She wrote down her number. And she was gone. And I... I should have gone with her, the hell with it. But I didn't. Because I do the right thing. I always do the right thing and yet I hardly ever feel good about it. I was standing in that room, in that house, strange people asleep everywhere. Suddenly it all became surreal.

LEYLA (*mumbles*). No... stop...

ANTON. Okay. Enough. It is time to go home.

GERRY. Hey! Easy. She's okay. She's fine, she's happy.

ANTON. She says – no.

GERRY. She doesn't mean it.

And he starts to laugh.

FELIX. Let's go. The man is right.

GERRY. Hey. As a matter of fact, I don't appreciate being thrown out. Is that how you treat your guests in Russia?

ANTON. I am not Russian.

FELIX. Gerry, come on... It was clear, we needed to get out as soon as possible. This man had had enough of us hours ago. If you could see Gerry, anybody would have kicked him out. Why then was I getting angry? The rage was starting to flood me out of nowhere. Who the hell do you think you are? I am doing the right thing, I am being respectful and considerate and generous... and you are kicking me out?!

GERRY. No, I want to know... and I mean, as a matter of fact, I was not ready to leave. And I think the girl, what's her name, should ask me to leave, if anyone should be asking me to leave.

FELIX. And the stupid idiot turned back –

ANTON. Hey. Go home.

GERRY. Go home. How about you go home?

ANTON. I can't.

GERRY. No one throws me out until I'm good and ready to go. And I'm not ready to go.

FELIX. Was I ready to go? Where was I going? Home? To a bed where Ann was going to hiss at me, half-asleep? Instead of standing here in the street I could be up there in a warm bed fucking a beautiful young woman who wanted me and would have been grateful and she… she…

GERRY. You think they're something special? I'll tell you something. There's a bathhouse, not very far from here actually, where girls like that kneel naked on all fours and serve as coffee tables. (*To* FELIX.) I'll take you.

Pause.

ANTON. I don't know who threw the first punch.

FELIX. I think I threw a punch, after I got one from… I think it might as well have been Gerry.

GERRY. I'm shit at punching but I do love it.

ANTON. I don't know where it came from. It wasn't so much the punch. They were babies.

GERRY. I couldn't tell.

FELIX. He slipped.

ANTON. Almost like in slow motion I staggered and I fell.

FELIX. And there was a crack. Like a coconut cracking.

ANTON. Like a walnut – the kind my father used to crack with a nutcracker. His big, wide, deeply lined palm opens in front of my face with pieces of sweet walnut core…

II

FELIX *sits alone at his table. He is wearing pyjamas and looks like he hasn't slept or had a bath in a few days.*

FELIX *stares intently into a spot on the table, his mind somewhere far away.*

The doorbell rings.

He opens the door. He takes a stunned step back. LARA *is at the door. He slams the door shut. Panic consumes him but he has to act quickly. He tries to collect himself and he opens the door again.*

LARA *is still there. If he could think clearly, he would notice she herself looks shocked. And very different from the other night. Pale, exhausted, like she hasn't slept a few days.*

Silence.

FELIX. What do you want?

LARA *stands in silence, looking for words.*

How did you find me? I didn't... did I? I didn't tell you where I lived, did I? I'm sure I didn't. Why would I? I mean, that's not what I mean, obviously...

He stops. An attempt at 'regrouping'.

LARA. Is your... wife here?

FELIX. No. No... she's gone.

LARA. Gone?

FELIX. For a few days. There's really no need to bring her into all this...

LARA. Well...

FELIX. I mean –

LARA. Can I come in?

FELIX. Yes. No! Erm…

He sighs, thinking frantically.

Yes, come in.

LARA *steps in. She looks around uncomfortably.*

More silence as they stare at each other.

Look, erm… obviously the part about my wife was somewhat unclear.

LARA. You didn't lie. You don't have a girlfriend.

FELIX. Yes. No, I don't.

More silence.

She's about to speak. He should let her speak. But he doesn't.

It's not really like that. At all. It's not.

LARA. Like what?

FELIX. Well, I'm… I'm a… a… I'm not like that.

LARA. Anton is in hospital.

FELIX. Is he?

LARA. Yes.

FELIX. Right.

Pause.

Is he going to be alright?

LARA. No.

FELIX *is distressed. He sits down.*

FELIX. It was an accident.

LARA. You…?

FELIX. No. (*Pause.*) I don't know.

She gazes at him intently.

(*A sudden burst of panic.*) What do you want from me? What do you want me to say? Do you know what you're asking from me? How am I supposed to explain what I was doing at your house with all of you and... Look. I know you must think I'm some sleazy Englishman who goes around picking up girls in clubs while his wife is sound asleep at home but I'm not. I've never done that sort of thing ever in my life. I mean not ever, ages ago, but not since I've been married. I don't do that!

LARA. You always take off your ring? When you go out?

He looks at the ring on his finger and covers it quickly, nervously, with his other hand.

FELIX. No... I... You don't understand. I work all the time, you see. I'm at my office. And when I'm not at my office, I'm at some office in some other country. And then when I'm not there, I'm at home with my wife, trying to... I haven't been to a club in... Spice Girls were a novelty the last time I've been to a club.

She doesn't laugh.

Gerry has a theory... about... turning into an alley... and there we were, and there you were, so incredibly pretty and glittery with that smile and that accent which is really quite...

He stops. He can't listen to himself.

He sighs deeply. An idea strikes him – almost like in a cartoon.

Coffee! I was just making coffee. Would you like a coffee? I think I need a coffee.

He goes to bring some coffee.

LARA. Okay.

FELIX *comes back with a box of biscuits.*

FELIX. Have a biscuit. There we go. They're very nice. Home-made. We get them at the farmers' market. So they're not actually home-made. They are. Just not this home. A home.

She takes a biscuit.

LARA. Ginger. I like ginger.

FELIX. Yes, it's nice, isn't it.

They sit while she eats her biscuit in silence.

LARA. Big table.

FELIX. Yes.

She puts a hand around her mouth and mimics yelling across the long table.

LARA. Pass the salt!

FELIX *laughs.*

Look, I –

FELIX. I just want to make it clear, if that's possible, that although I got carried away that night, I meant everything I said to you and I am usually never that forward –

Her expression suggests that was not what she would call particularly forward.

… Oh, for fuck's sake, what is happening? Everything seems to be tumbling down, do you know that feeling?

LARA. Yes.

FELIX *rubs his head, his face distorted with frustration.*

FELIX. I don't know why I behaved like I behaved… You did come on to me, though?

LARA. Sorry?

FELIX. Yes. 'You look familiar,' if that's not a pick-up line –

LARA. You do look familiar.

FELIX. Oh, yeah? How is that?

LARA. Well –

FELIX. I trusted you, you know, in fact, curiously, I trusted you completely where I had no good cause to trust you at all. I mean, I read the book!

LARA. What book?

FELIX. The Tractor book. The history of... what you call it...

LARA. What?

FELIX. Never mind. It's very hot, don't you find?

He takes his robe off fervently.

Is your name Lara?

LARA. Yes! Larisa, actually.

FELIX. Well, I can tell you one thing, Larisa, I don't appreciate being ambushed like this in my own home. (*Pause.*) I mean –

Pause.

LARA. I didn't seduce you.

Pause. He listens.

I liked you.

FELIX. Really?

LARA. Really.

He smiles.

FELIX. I liked you. I really did.

LARA. You were funny. You are funny when you're drunk.

He blushes.

FELIX. I had such a good time. Honestly. I can't remember...

She doesn't share his degree of enthusiasm.

You don't think?

LARA. It was fun, yes.

FELIX. You do that sort of thing often?

LARA. Have fun?

FELIX. ... Well, yes.

LARA takes a little while to think about it.

LARA. I think... yes, I think we have fun.

He ponders.

You don't have fun?

FELIX. I do. I... I do. We go to dinners with friends. To a... a sushi place most often. We... like sushi. And we go to Battersea Park on Sundays. Sometimes. Picnics. Loads of fun. We have loads of fun.

LARA. I don't like sushi.

FELIX. No?

LARA. No. It's cold and wet. Food shouldn't be cold and wet.

FELIX. Well, if you put it that way...

LARA. It's true.

FELIX. When I said I'd call... Truth is, I probably wouldn't have... called. Because... well, as you can see... and um... But the truth is... when I said I'd call, when I asked if I can call, I wanted to. I really wanted to. In fact, I wanted to see if you would say yes.

LARA. Did you think I would say no?

FELIX. Yeah!

LARA. Why?

FELIX. Well, you're millions of years younger than me for one. And you're really gorgeous! And I'm...

LARA. You were sweet.

FELIX (*disappointed*). Sweet.

LARA. Sweet. And kind. A little clumsy maybe. Different. I never met anyone like you. I mean, not like a friend. And you didn't try to fuck me. You were just interested. And you were drunk. Not many of people are interested in other people when they are drunk.

He considers. That's a compliment he never got before.

So yes, I would like you to call me. (*Pause.*) But you can't.

Now she indicates 'all this'.

FELIX. I'm so sorry. You have to believe me.

She doesn't give much away.

It was a stupid impulse to take off the ring. I don't know what came over me. You must believe me.

LARA. I believe you.

He is relieved. But not for long.

I go sit with him in the hospital. I don't know. Maybe he can't hear me. But I think maybe yes. And I say – don't worry. He is a good man. I know. I can feel that. He will come.

FELIX. I… I don't think I am. Really. I… I see other people coping really well, in fact, they even seem to be having a good time. Then I think it must all be a lie, surely, and if I could only cut through it – but I can't even do that with my own wife. I feel bruised by people all the time. You seemed to listen but the price is awfully fucking high. And I have no more patience. The bullshit quota has been filled to the brim! But what can I do? I have no power in this world, I don't make decisions. I feel like a bug turned on its back, desperately trying to flip over. I live a sorry existence at the expense of other people. At your expense and all those people I shall never see nor meet. I give money to the beggars although I feel ambivalent about it, I give money to the charities although I know that only helps to maintain a status quo. I am a member of Amnesty International and I usually don't have time to read their bulletin that comes in the post. I want to act and I don't know where to start. I want to make a difference and I don't believe in making a difference. I dread signing any forms, I don't trust anyone because people tend to 'reinvent' themselves way too often to actually be reliable at what they do. I recycle, not always, not everything. Not the jars with bits of herbs and pickles left at the bottom. I buy organic and I want to buy local but it's virtually impossible to find green beans that don't come from Kenya. I do what I can and it's all insignificant and I am tired. I am tired. I don't have the courage to pick up and leave. I don't have the courage to start life over and I don't even know where that would be. I am as helpless and exhausted as a bug that's given up on trying to flip over.

Pause.

I always thought I was the kind of guy who steps up. And it turns out, I'm the man that looks away.

A long half of a minute goes by. FELIX *picks up the phone.*

Yes. Hi, could you connect me to the Shoreditch Police Station please?

She watches him as he waits, not looking at her.

Hello? Hi. My name is Felix Wells. I… have some information about the serious assault that took place the other night in Packington Street. (*Pause.*) Yes, my address is 38 St John Street, EC1 NL5. (*Pause.*) Yes, I could come in. Yes, midday would be fine. Thank you. Goodbye.

He puts the phone down.

LARA. Thank you.

He is relieved.

Silence. He sinks into the sofa.

LARA *starts to feel jittery and awkward.*

I think… I should maybe…

She chuckles. Nervously. She gets up. He looks at her as if he has just woken up from a bad dream.

FELIX. Are you going?

LARA. No… I don't know.

FELIX. I suppose… well, I don't know either.

She hovers uncomfortably.

What?

LARA. I'm your cleaner.

Pause.

I'm your cleaner.

Pause.

I clean your flat.

FELIX. What? No. Our cleaner… she is Polish, I think. And old. I think.

LARA. No. That was one before me. About one month ago.

Pause.

FELIX. We got a new cleaner. 'She's great. Quite cute. Good thing you're not around.'

Silence.

LARA. I didn't… find you. I just… came to work.

FELIX. You said you were a designer. And a waitress.

LARA. I am. Waitress too. Designer, one day. If I say I am a cleaner… You wouldn't…

He looks up. Ready to protest. But he doesn't. Because he wouldn't, she's right. She points to the kitchen.

You have that picture on the fridge. You and your wife. I just remembered. That's why you look familiar.

Silence.

Not very many pictures around. Just that one.

Silence.

FELIX. You didn't come to …

LARA. No.

FELIX. And you only asked about my wife because of…

LARA. Yes.

Silence.

Do you want me to leave?

FELIX, *exhausted, sinks into a chair.*

FELIX. I don't know.

*

A police siren is heard.

*

At the long kitchen table.

ANN. What have you done?

Silence.

What have you done to us?

FELIX. It just happened.

ANN. Will you go to prison?

FELIX. I don't know.

ANN. Will you be fired?

FELIX. I don't know.

ANN. How can you be so calm? Why the hell weren't you so calm when the little witch called? (*Pause.*) Felix, between them and us, couldn't you have picked us?

Silence.

FELIX. I can't ask you to understand. I can't take back what I said. I can't undo what's been done. (*Pause.*) It happened. I had to find out.

ANN. Find out what?

A Hospital

ANTON *lies in a hospital bed, hooked to a machine, unconscious.*

LARA *sits next to him.*

LARA. I told you, didn't I?

Pause.

The hero... The hero met with his destiny. What was he trying to do? Did he want to protect the young woman? Did she need protecting? Did he think his household was under threat? The place he never used to see as his home. And what of the young woman and her story? A woman deserves more than just to be the wife of a man who works his whole life to be able to afford a funeral. Don't you think? The young woman continued to search for happiness. Though she couldn't really say she'd ever met anyone who'd found it. But as she travelled the world, happiness changed face.

Once the woes of the world penetrated her heart, she was no longer capable of going back to a place where the happiness she imagined would be possible. But on her journey one man loved her and she will carry this love with her for ever. And another man, he might have loved her if it had been her dream. So she was confident that there will be more love along the way. The wind won't blow her away. Her life will have a meaning.

The End.

A Nick Hern Book

Invisible first published in Great Britain as a paperback original in 2011 by Nick Hern Books Limited, 14 Larden Road, London W3 7ST, in association with the New Wolsey Theatre, Ipswich, and Transport

Invisible copyright © 2011 Tena Štivičić

Tena Štivičić has asserted her right to be identified as the author of this work

Cover photograph: Zbigniew Kotkiewicz
Cover design: Ned Hoste 2H

Typeset by Nick Hern Books, London
Printed in Great Britain by Mimeo Ltd, St Ives, Cambs PE27 3LE

A CIP catalogue record for this book is available from the British Library

ISBN   978 1 84842 236 0